STECK-VAUGHN
GED

The Essay

PROGRAM CONSULTANTS

Myra K. Baum
New York, New York

Sheron Lee Chic
Community School South
East Palo Alto, California

June E. Dean
Parent and Adult Education
Detroit Public Schools
Detroit, Michigan

Ruth E. Derfler, M.Ed.
State GED Chief Examiner
Massachusetts Department of
    Education
Malden, Massachusetts

Joan S. Flanery
Adult Education and Literacy
    Program
Ashland Independent Board
    of Education
Ashland, Kentucky

Michael E. Snyder, Ed.S.
Tennessee Department of
    Corrections
Pikeville, Tennessee

STECK-VAUGHN
C O M P A N Y
ELEMENTARY • SECONDARY • ADULT • LIBRARY

Staff Credits

Executive Editor:	Ellen Northcutt
Senior Editor:	Tim Collins
Design Manager:	John J. Harrison
Cover Design:	Rhonda Childress
Photo Editor:	Margie Foster
Photography:	Cover: (Gettysburg) © Paul Conklin/Uniphoto.
	All photography © James Minor.
Contributing Writers:	James W. Beers
	J. Thomas Gill, Jr.

ISBN 0-8114-7362-7

Copyright © 1996 Steck-Vaughn Company.

Printed in the United States of America.

2 3 4 5 6 7 8 9 BP 00 99 98 97 96

Contents

To the Learner

What Is the GED Test?

You are taking a very big step toward changing your life with your decision to take the GED test. By opening this book, you are taking your second important step: preparing for the test. You may feel nervous about what is ahead, which is only natural. Relax and read the following pages to find out the answers to your questions.

The GED test, the Test of General Educational Development, is given by the GED Testing Service of the American Council on Education for adults who did not graduate from high school. When you pass the GED test, you will receive a certificate that is regarded as equivalent to a high school diploma. Employers in private industry and government, as well as admissions officers in colleges and universities, accept the GED certificate as they would a high school diploma.

The GED test covers the same subjects people study in high school. The five subject areas are: Writing Skills, Interpreting Literature and the Arts, Social Studies, Science, and Mathematics. You will not be required to know all the information that is usually taught in high school. You will, however, be tested on your ability to read and process information. Certain U.S. states also require a test on the U.S. Constitution or on state government. Check with your local adult education center to see if your state requires such a test.

Each year hundreds of thousands of adults pass the GED test. The *Steck-Vaughn GED Series* will help you develop and refine the reading, writing, and thinking skills you need to pass the GED test.

GED Scores

After you complete the GED test, you will get a score for each section and a total score. The total score is an average of all the other scores. The highest score possible on a single test is 80. The scores needed to pass the GED test vary depending on where you live. The chart on page 3 shows the minimum state requirements. A score of *40 or 45* means that the score for each test must be 40 or more, but if one or more scores is below 40, an average of at least 45 is required. A minimum score of *35 and 45* means that the score for each test must be 35 or more and an average of at least 45 is required.

GED Score Requirements

Area	Minimum Score on Each Test		Minimum Average on All Five Tests
UNITED STATES			
Alabama, Alaska, Arizona, Connecticut, Georgia, Hawaii, Illinois, Indiana, Iowa, Kansas, Kentucky, Maine, Massachusetts, Michigan, Minnesota, Montana,Nevada, New Hampshire, North Carolina, Ohio, Pennsylvania, Rhode Island, South Carolina, Tennessee, Vermont, Virginia, Wyoming	35	and	45
Arkansas, California, Colorado, Delaware, District of Columbia, Florida, Idaho, Maryland, Missouri, New York, Oklahoma, Oregon, South Dakota, Utah, Washington, West Virginia	40	and	45
Louisiana, Mississippi, Nebraska, New Mexico, North Dakota, Texas	40	or	45
New Jersey (42 is required on Test 1; 40 is required on Tests 2, 3, and 4; 45 is required on Test 5; and 45 average on all 5 tests.)			
Wisconsin	40	and	50
CANADA			
Alberta, British Columbia, Manitoba, New Brunswick (English and French), Northwest Territories, Nova Scotia, Prince Edward Island, Saskatchewan, Yukon Territory	45		—
Newfoundland	40	and	45
U.S. TERRITORIES & OTHERS			
Guam, Kwajalein, Puerto Rico, Virgin Islands	35	and	45
Panama Canal Area, Palau	40	and	45
Mariana Islands, Marshall Islands, Micronesia	40	or	45
American Samoa	40		—

Note: GED score requirements change from time to time. For the most up-to-date information, check with your state or local GED director or GED testing center.

This chart gives you information on the content, number of items, and time limit for each test. In some places you do not have to take all sections of the test on the same day. If you want to take all the test sections in one day, the GED test will last an entire day. Check with your local adult education center for the requirements in your area.

Test	Content Areas	Number of Items	Time Limit (minutes)
Writing Skills Part I	Sentence Structure Usage Mechanics	55	75
Writing Skills Part II	Essay	1	45
Social Studies	Geography U.S. History Economics Political Science Behavioral Science	64	85
Science	Biology Earth Science Physics Chemistry	66	95
Interpreting Literature and the Arts	Popular Literature Classical Literature Commentary	45	65
Mathematics	Arithmetic Algebra Geometry	56	90

≡Where Do You Go to Take the GED Test?

The GED test is offered year-round throughout the United States, its possessions, U.S. military bases worldwide, and in Canada. To find out when and where tests are held near you, contact the GED Hot Line at 1-800-62-MY-GED (1-800-626-9433) or one of these institutions in your area:

- ♦ An adult education center
- ♦ A continuing education center
- ♦ A local community college
- ♦ A public library

- ♦ A private business school or technical school
- ♦ The public board of education

In addition, the Hot Line and the institutions can give you information regarding necessary identification, testing fees, and writing implements. Schedules vary: some testing centers are open several days a week; others are open only on weekends.

Why Should You Take the GED Test?

A GED certificate can help you in the following ways:

Employment

People without high school diplomas or GED certificates have much more difficulty changing jobs or moving up in their present companies. In many cases employers will not hire someone who does not have a high school diploma or the equivalent.

Education

If you want to enroll in a technical school, a vocational school, or an apprenticeship program, you often must have a high school diploma or the equivalent. If you want to enter a college or university, you must have a high school diploma or the equivalent.

Personal

The most important thing is how you feel about yourself. You have the unique opportunity to turn back the clock by making something happen that did not happen in the past. You can attain a GED certificate that will help you in the future and make you feel better about yourself now.

How to Prepare for the GED Test

Classes for GED preparation are available to anyone who wants to take the GED. The choice of whether to take classes is up to you; they are not required. If you prefer to study by yourself, the *Steck-Vaughn GED Series* has been prepared to guide your study. *Steck-Vaughn GED Exercise Books* are also available to give you additional practice for each test.

Most GED preparation programs offer individualized instruction and tutors who can help you identify areas in which you may need help. Many adult education centers offer free day or night classes. The classes are usually informal and allow you to work at your own pace and with other adults who also are studying for the GED. In addition to working on specific skills, you will be able to take practice GED tests (like those in this book) in order to check your progress. For information about classes available near you, contact one of the institutions in the list on page 4.

Passing Test One: Part II, The Essay

In Test One, Part II you will be asked to write an essay. An essay is a composition of more than one paragraph that gives the writer's views on a particular topic. This book will teach you effective ways to gather and organize ideas, write your essay, evaluate it, and revise it. You will focus on developing a five-paragraph essay, which is an effective way to organize a GED essay. A five-paragraph essay includes an introductory paragraph, three body paragraphs, and a conclusion paragraph.

The Writing Assignment

The essay topic assignment will be brief. You will be asked to "state a view," "present an opinion," or "explain why or how" about an issue or situation familiar to adults. You will be expected to write an essay of about 200 words that clearly explains your point of view. You will not need any specialized knowledge or information to respond to the topic. A typical topic assignment, for example, might ask you to describe the effects of the automobile on modern life.

The directions for the essay test tell you the steps to take to prepare your answer. You will be allowed 45 minutes to complete your essay. A sample essay topic and directions are on page 7.

How Will Your Essay Be Scored?

Your essay will be scored holistically. This means that it will be judged on its overall effectiveness. If you misspell a few words or make a few grammatical errors, your composition will not get a failing score. However, if you make so many of these errors that your ideas are hard to understand, your score will go down. What is most important is how well you stick to the topic and how well you support your topic with examples.

Two different people will score your essay. Each one will read your essay and decide how effective it is based on its content, organization, and control of the English language. Each scorer will use the GED Essay Scoring Guide (see page 8) and assign a score ranging from 1 to 6. The two scores are then added, resulting in a range of scores from 2 to 12. A third scorer will be used if the first two scores are more than one point apart.

The scores you earn on Test One: Writing Skills, Parts I and II will be combined and reported as a single score on a standard score scale.

Sample GED Essay Test

TEST ONE: WRITING SKILLS TEST, PART II

Tests of General Educational Development Writing Skills, Part Two

Instructions

This is a test to find out how well you write. The test has one question which asks you to present an opinion on an issue or to explain something. In preparing your answer for this question, you should take the following steps:

1. Read all of the information accompanying the question.

2. Plan your answer carefully before you write.

3. Use the blank pages of this test booklet (or scratch paper) to make any notes.

4. Write your answer on the separate answer sheet.

5. Read carefully what you have written and make any changes that will improve your writing.

6. Check your paragraphing, sentence structure, spelling, punctuation, capitalization, and usage, and make any necessary corrections.

You will have 45 minutes to write on the question you are assigned. Write legibly and use a ball point pen so that evaluators will be able to read your writing. The notes you make on the blank pages (scratch paper) will not be scored. Your composition will be scored by at least two trained evaluators who will judge the paper according to its overall effectiveness. They will be concerned with how clearly you make the main point of your composition, how thoroughly you support your ideas, and how clear and correct your writing is throughout the composition. You will receive no credit for writing on a question other than the one assigned.

SAMPLE TOPIC

The automobile has certainly been responsible for many changes in the United States. Some of these changes have improved our lives and some have made life more difficult or unpleasant.

Write a composition of about 200 words describing the effect of the automobile on modern life. You may describe the positive effects, the negative effects, or both. Be specific, and use examples to support your view.

All actual essay topics used with GED examinees are secure and not available in print. However, on the following pages we are able to provide the GED Testing Service's Essay Scoring Guide, a sample essay written by a high school senior, and the essay's score.

Reprinted with permission of the American Council on Education.

GED Essay Scoring Guide

GED Essay Scoring Guide

Copyright © 1987, GED Testing Service

Papers will show *some or all* of the following characteristics.

Upper-half papers have a clear, definite purpose pursued with varying degrees of effectiveness. They have a structure that shows evidence of some deliberate planning. The writer's control of the conventions of Standard Written English (spelling, punctuation, grammar, word choice, and sentence structure) ranges from fairly reliable at 4 to confident and accomplished at 6.

6　The *6 paper* offers sophisticated ideas within an organizational framework that is clear and appropriate for the topic. The supporting statements are particularly effective because of their substance, specificity, or illustrative quality. The writing is vivid and precise, although it may contain an occasional error in the conventions of Standard Written English.

5　The *5 paper* is clearly organized with effective support for each of the writer's major points. While the writing offers substantive ideas, it lacks the fluency found in the *6 paper*. Although there are some errors, the conventions of Standard English are consistently under control.

4　The *4 paper* shows evidence of the writer's organizational plan. Support, though adequate, tends to be less extensive or effective than that found in the *5 paper*. The writer generally observes the conventions of Standard Written English. The errors that are present are not severe enough to interfere significantly with the writer's main purpose.

Lower-half papers either fail to convey a purpose sufficiently or lack one entirely. Consequently, their structure ranges from rudimentary at 3, to random at 2, to absent at 1. Control of the conventions of Standard Written English tends to follow this same gradient.

3　The *3 paper* usually shows some evidence of planning, although the development is insufficient. The supporting statements may be limited to a listing or a repetition of ideas. The *3 paper* often demonstrates repeated weaknesses in the conventions of Standard Written English.

2　The *2 paper* is characterized by a marked lack of organization or inadequate support for ideas. The development is usually superficial or unfocused. Errors in the conventions of Standard Written English may seriously interfere with the overall effectiveness of this paper.

1　The *1 paper* lacks purpose or development. The dominant feature is the absence of control of structure or the conventions of Standard Written English. The deficiencies are so severe that the writer's ideas are difficult or impossible to understand.

*　An asterisk code is reserved for papers that are blank, illegible, or written on a topic other than the one assigned. Because these papers cannot be scored, a Writing Skills Test composite score cannot be reported.

To the Learner

Sample Essay

~~The invention of the automobile has certainly done more good for more people~~

The good that the invention of the automobile has done for the world, in terms of convenience, time and labor, certainly outweighs the problems it has caused. The invention ~~invention~~ of the automobile has created a tremendous job market in the united states and other auto manufacturing countries. What's more, It ~~was~~ the need for fuel to operate all the cars, trucks, and motorcycles on the road today has helped to ~~create~~ create thriving, modern countries where backward & third-world countries were once predominate.

On a smaller scale, the automobile has tremendously benefited such people as farmers, who can transport goods much quicker today than just a century ago. Productivity in a variety of businesses has increased because important materials and information can be delivered in hours where it used to take days or weeks. Moreover, treatment of the sick or injured is now more efficient because necessary machinery or medicines can be rapidly obtained, not to mention the fact that patients themselves can be transported to hospitals much more quickly: A ~~tremendous~~ great benefit. where time can be the difference between life or death.

Even with all the ~~good~~ services that automobiles provide, there are still some major drawbacks. Some of these, like accidents due to faulty construction, are being slowly but surely removed as science and technology advances. Others, such as drunk driving, may never be eliminated, but their frequencies can certainly be lessened as public awareness and outcry increases.

There are other problems, too; how automobiles affect the ecology of our planet, dense traffic, increasing hazards due to increasing driver population, to name a few. All of these however, ~~do not solve~~ are not reasons to oppose ~~the~~ automobile production. As described, automobiles are not only beneficial but necessary to today's world. These problems will just have to be dealt with in time.

Commentary on the Sample Essay

The actual scorers both gave the sample essay the score of 6 using the GED Essay Scoring Guide. This is how they explained the score:

The opening sentence of the paper is distinctive in its statement of an assertion at the same time that it imposes a principle of organization on the writing that follows. The writer provides adequate and convincing support for the assertion, and goes beyond the bounds of normal expectations through the rhetorical technique of refuting the arguments that oppose the assertion. The essay is by no means perfect—the writer exhibits some confusion over the use of the semicolon, for example—but it shows writing that is consistently smooth and confident, even elegant. It is worth noting, too, that the paper is no longer than many efforts of lesser distinction.

The POWER Writing Program

By helping you focus on passing the GED Writing Skills Test, Part II and by giving you a step-by-step approach to writing a good five-paragraph essay, this book gives you the POWER to succeed. In fact, we call our program the POWER Program. Each step—from how to begin your essay to how to end it—is listed for you. **P** stands for **Plan, O** for **Organize, W** for **Write, E** for **Evaluate,** and **R** for **Revise.** The chart that follows summarizes the POWER Writing Program.

POWER STEPS

	Chapter	Steps	Time
P	**Planning Your Essay** (p. 14–23)	☐ Figure out the topic. ☐ Understand the instructions. ☐ Choose your main idea. ☐ Gather ideas.	5 minutes
O	**Organizing Your Essay** (p. 24–35)	☐ Group and name your ideas. ☐ Expand your groups. ☐ Order your groups.	5 minutes
W	**Writing Your Essay** (p. 36–53)	☐ Write your introduction. ☐ Write your body paragraphs. ☐ Write your conclusion.	25 minutes
E	**Evaluating Your Essay** (p. 54–71)	☐ Evaluate your ideas and organization. ☐ Evaluate your use of the conventions of English.	5 minutes
R	**Revising Your Essay** (p. 72–81)	☐ Revise your ideas and organization. ☐ Revise your use of the conventions of English.	5 minutes

In this book you will get plenty of practice with each of the POWER steps. Review the POWER steps until they become automatic for you and use them as you write the essays in this book. Following the time limits will allow sufficient time for you to write a good essay and check it within the 45-minute time limit on the test.

Study Skills

Study Regularly

- If you can, set aside an hour to study every day. If you do not have time every day, set up a schedule of the days you can study. Be sure to pick times when you will be the most relaxed and least likely to be bothered by outside distractions.

- Let others know your study time. Ask them to leave you alone for that period. It helps if you explain to others why this is important.

- You should be relaxed when you study, so find an area that is comfortable for you. If you cannot study at home, go to the library. Most public libraries have areas for reading and studying. If there is a college or university near you, find out if you can use its library. All libraries have dictionaries, encyclopedias, and other resources you can use if you need more information while you're studying.

Organize Your Study Materials

- Be sure to have pens, sharp pencils, and paper.

- Keep all of your books together. If you are taking an adult education class, you probably will be able to borrow some books or other study material.

- Make a notebook or folder for each subject you are studying. Folders with pockets are useful for storing loose papers.

- Keep all of your material in one place so you do not waste time looking for it each time you study.

Read Regularly

- Read the newspaper, read magazines, read books. Read whatever appeals to you—but read! Regular, daily reading is the best way to improve your reading skills.

Write Regularly

- Try to write every day. The more you write, the more comfortable you will feel writing. You will receive extensive practice in the units of this book, the Simulated GED Tests on pages 114–115, and the Additional GED Topics on pages 116–117. In addition, some learners find that keeping a journal or writing letters to friends in other cities or countries gives valuable writing experience.

Taking the Test

Before the Test

♦ If you have never been to the test center, go there the day before the test. If you drive, find out where to park. This way you won't get lost the day of the test.

♦ Prepare the things you need for the test: your admission ticket (if necessary), acceptable identification, some pens and sharpened No. 2 pencils with erasers, a watch, glasses, a jacket or sweater (in case the room is cold), and a snack to eat during breaks.

♦ You will do your best work if you are rested and alert. So do not cram before the test. Instead, eat a meal and get a good night's sleep. If the test is early in the morning, set the alarm.

The Day of the Test

♦ Eat a good breakfast. Wear comfortable clothing. Make sure that you have all of the materials you need.

♦ Try to arrive at the test center about twenty minutes early. This allows time if, for example, there is a last-minute change of room.

♦ If you are going to be at the test center all day, you might pack a lunch. If you have to find a restaurant or if you wait a long time to be served, you may be late for the rest of the test.

Using this Book

♦ You can work through the units in this book in any order, or you can focus on only the units you need to review. However, for the best results, we recommend that you complete all the units in order. Use Simulated Tests A and B to decide if you are ready for the real test.

♦ If you are taking a class, have your teacher evaluate your essays. If you are working independently, ask a friend or relative to read your essays. If this is not possible, evaluate your writing yourself. After finishing an essay, put it aside for a day. Then read it as objectively as possible. No matter who checks your writing, make sure that person uses the chart on page 8 and the check list on page 120 as scoring/evaluation guides.

♦ Write the date on your completed essays and keep them together in a folder or notebook. This way, you will be able to track your progress, note your strengths, and figure out areas in which you want to improve.

Unit 1 PLANNING

P	**Planning** Your Essay
O Organizing Your Essay	◆ **Figuring Out the Topic** ◆ **Understanding the Instructions** ◆ **Choosing Your Main Idea** ◆ **Gathering Ideas**
W Writing Your Essay	
E Evaluating Your Essay	
R Revising Your Essay	

The first step of the POWER writing process is planning. To write a good GED essay, you have to write about the assigned topic and include a lot of good ideas. In Unit 1, you will learn how to plan your essay so that it is about the assigned topic and includes a variety of good ideas.

Figuring Out the Topic

The GED Writing Test, Part II, begins with the **writing assignment.** Completing a GED writing assignment does not require any specialized information or knowledge. Rather, the GED requires you to state your opinion. Your composition has to back up this opinion with specific examples drawn from your experience.

For example, a writing assignment on seat belt laws would not ask how many people die each year in traffic accidents because they were not wearing seat belts. Instead, it would ask whether you think that laws requiring people to wear seat belts are a good idea.

A GED writing assignment contains three parts:
◆ Background information on the topic
◆ The topic
◆ The instructions

Here is a typical GED writing assignment with the parts marked:

Background information on the topic — Recently several states have passed laws requiring the driver and passengers in a motor vehicle to wear seat belts while the vehicle is in operation. Many people believe that these laws infringe on personal freedom. Others believe that these laws are necessary to save lives. — **Use the background information to give you ideas about the topic.**

The topic—the subject of your essay — Write a composition of about 200 words that explains your opinion about (laws requiring the use of seat belts.) Tell why you agree or disagree with the seat belt laws. Be specific and use examples to support your views. — **All of the ideas in your essay should relate to this topic.**

The instructions —what you are to do — **The instructions state the kind of information you need to give in your essay.**

Notice, first, that writing about the **topic** does not require any specialized information, but instead requires your opinion about seat belt laws. Notice, too, how the **background information** gives you ideas about possible opinions you might talk about in your essay. You might agree with the laws because they save lives. You might disagree with the laws because you think that they interfere with people's personal freedom.

Also, notice how the **instructions** clearly state the kind of information required. The instructions ask you to agree or disagree and give specific examples to back up this opinion.

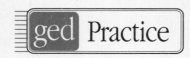

Figuring Out the Topic

Read each GED writing assignment. Draw a box around the background information, circle the topic, and underline the instructions.

TOPIC 1

Because of the increase of women in the work force, finding ways to arrange adequate child care has become a major issue. To address the problem, many companies have begun to provide on-site day care for their employees' children.

Write a composition of about 200 words discussing whether or not you think employers should supply child care for their employees. Be specific and use examples to support your view.

TOPIC 2

Mandatory drug testing in the work place has been the cause for heated debate. Many people feel that testing employees is an invasion of privacy. Others see it as a way of protecting themselves and their employees.

In a composition of about 200 words, describe the effects of mandatory drug testing on employees. You may wish to describe the positive effects, the negative effects, or both. Use specific examples to support your opinion.

TOPIC 3

Most jobs today require applicants to have either a GED or a high-school diploma. For many employers, these certificates are evidence of the applicant's ability to accomplish goals and perform at certain standards.

How important is having a GED or a high-school diploma when you apply for a job? In an essay of about 200 words, tell your opinion. Use specific examples to support your view.

TOPIC 4

Although cigarette ads were banned from TV in the 1970s, they still appear in magazines and on billboards. Many ads seem to appeal to an even younger audience.

In an essay of about 200 words, tell how you think cigarette advertising should be handled. Should all ads for cigarettes be banned? Support your opinion with specific examples.

Understanding the Instructions

The instructions in the writing assignment tell you how to write your essay. It is important to understand exactly what the instructions say. Usually, **key words** in the instructions will help you understand what to write.

This chart contains some of the key words that are used in GED writing instructions and tells the kind of information you should give in your composition.

Understanding the Instructions	
If the Instructions Say:	**You Should:**
1. describe the effect of... tell how this might affect...	write about causes and effects

2. explain how or why...
    tell how...
    discuss...
    identify...
    describe how...
    describe why...
	give reasons or explain facts about an issue

3. state a view...
    present an opinion...
    state your opinion...
	tell what you think about an issue

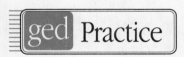 Practice Understanding the Instructions

Read each GED writing assignment. Underline the instructions. Use the chart to figure out the kind of information your essay should provide. Write the kind of information on the line.

TOPIC 1

Fast food is a part of our way of life. Fast-food restaurants can be found all over the country selling hamburgers, chicken, and fish sandwiches. Many of these places have inexpensive salad bars, too.

Why are fast-food restaurants so popular today? In a composition of 200 words, state the reasons for fast food's popularity. Support your opinion with specific examples.

---

tell what you think about an issue

TOPIC 2

Airplanes are the fastest way to get from one place to another. Today you can eat breakfast in Chicago, lunch in Dallas, and dinner in Los Angeles. For many people this is a modern miracle, but others are afraid that rapid transportation may have negative effects on daily life.

Write a composition of 200 words that describes both the negative and the positive effects of rapid transportation on everyday life. Be specific and use examples.

TOPIC 3

In many families, both parents work outside the home. Children under the age of five are cared for by full-time baby-sitters or in day-care centers until they are old enough to go to school.

Is it harmful for both parents of a preschool child to work outside the home? In a composition of about 200 words, state your opinion. Use specific examples to support your point of view.

TOPIC 4

Climates vary greatly in different parts of the country. Some people say that they would not move to a certain place because of the effect the weather would have on their lives.

How does the climate where you live affect you and the people who live there? Write a composition of about 200 words describing the good points, the bad points, or both. Be specific, and use examples to support your views.

TOPIC 5

Young people spend as much as five or six hours a day watching TV. Anything that takes up so much of their time will affect them—for good or for bad.

In a composition of 200 words, describe the effects on young people of watching TV. You may describe good or bad effects, or both. Be specific, and use examples to support your views.

Choosing Your Main Idea

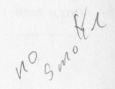

After you figure out the topic and understand the instructions, you can begin planning your response. First, you need to choose your main idea. The **main idea** is the opinion you want to present in your essay. For example, a composition on the topic of seat belt laws can be either for or against the laws. If you are for seat belt laws, your main idea might be, "Laws making seat belts mandatory have many advantages."

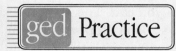 Practice   Choosing Your Main Idea

Read each writing assignment. Circle the topic. Then write a main idea for it.

TOPIC 1

Some people like the fast-paced life and activity of the city, while others believe that the peace and quiet of a small town offer the ideal life.

In a composition of about 200 words, discuss (whether you think life is better in the country or in the city.) Give specific reasons for your choice.

Main idea: _Living in the city has given me several benefits._

TOPIC 2

Drug testing in the workplace is the basis for heated debate. Many people think testing is an invasion of privacy. Others see it as a way to protect themselves and other employees.

In a composition of 200 words, describe the effects of drug testing on employees. You may describe positive effects, negative effects, or both. Use specific examples.

Main idea: _____

TOPIC 3

Most jobs require applicants to have a GED or a high-school diploma. These certificates are evidence of an applicant's ability to accomplish goals and perform at certain standards.

How important is it to have a GED or a high-school diploma when you apply for a job? In a composition of about 200 words, state your view. Use specific examples for support.

Main idea: _____

Gathering Ideas

All the ideas you gather should support your essay's main idea.

Once you have a main idea, you are ready to begin **gathering ideas** for your essay. This is a very important step because you need to back up your main idea with a variety of examples. An easy way to gather ideas is to think about the main idea and then start listing as many related ideas as you can.

You may worry that you won't be able to think of enough ideas to write a good essay. A good way to overcome this fear is by relaxing and writing all of the ideas that come to mind—as many as you can. The best ideas you get may not be the first ideas you think of, so don't stop with two or three ideas. If you write only a few ideas, you're stuck with those. If you write down a lot of ideas, you can pick and choose the best.

A good habit to get into when you are thinking about ideas is to make a note of the time you begin. Allow yourself at least five minutes to think of and write ideas. When you have written as many ideas as you can, stop and look at them. Are there enough ideas to work with?

Two good ways to write your ideas are lists and idea maps. When you make a **list,** you write the ideas in the order you think of them. When you make an **idea map,** you write down ideas in a way that shows their relationship to the main idea.

Look at how two students wrote their ideas about seat belt laws. One student wrote a list and the other wrote an idea map.

Student 1's List

Main Idea: *Seat belt laws are good.*

— *save lives*

— *people are more careful*

— *cities make money on fines*

— *people would not use them*

Student 2's Idea Map

can't get out of car after accident

Main Idea: Seat belt laws are bad.

people should make their own decisions

government controls too much

Read each main idea. Then write a list of ideas about it.

1. Digital pagers and portable telephones have changed how we communicate in several ways.

2. Some kinds of popular music are bad influences on young people.

3. Universal, free health care is a good idea.

4. It's very important to have a GED or a high-school diploma when you apply for a job.

 Writing Idea Maps

Read each main idea. Then write an idea map about it.

For extra help in making your idea maps, write your idea maps on copies of the blank idea map on page 119.

1. Watching too much television is bad for people.

2. People spend too much money on their pets.

3. Life in the city has advantages over life in the country.

4. The government should encourage people to use public transportation.

A. Read the GED writing assignment. Draw a box around the background information, circle the topic, and underline the instructions.

> Over the past few years, many people who were living in the country have moved to the city. At the same time, many people in the city have moved to the country.
>
> In a composition of about 200 words, state whether you think life is better in the country or in the city. Give specific examples to support your view.

B. Look at the instructions. What kind of information is required? Write the kind of information.

_____

_____

C. Look at the topic and the background information. Then think of a main idea for an essay on this topic. Write your main idea.

_____

_____

D. Think about the main idea you wrote in C. Then write a list of ideas or an idea map about it.

_____

For extra help in making your idea map, write your idea map on a copy of the blank idea map on page 119.

_____

ORGANIZING

P Planning Your Essay

O Organizing Your Essay

- ◆ **Grouping and Naming Your Ideas**
- ◆ **Expanding Your Groups**
- ◆ **Ordering Your Groups**

W Writing Your Essay

E Evaluating Your Essay

R Revising Your Essay

The second step in the POWER writing process is organizing your ideas for writing. Organization is one of the features of good writing. In this unit, you will learn how to divide your ideas into three groups. You'll also see how to add ideas to your groups. Finally, you'll put your idea groups in a logical order.

Grouping and Naming Your Ideas

Once you have some ideas about a topic, your next step is **grouping and naming ideas.** Each group of ideas will become a paragraph to support the main idea of your essay. To group ideas, see what the ideas in your list have in common. Put related ideas in a group and label or name the group to show how they relate to the main idea. Then group the next related ideas and label them. If an idea doesn't fit in any group, cross it out.

Here is the way one student grouped her ideas about the effects of watching TV.

Main idea: Watching TV has both good and bad effects.

The Effects of Watching TV
violence seems to be everywhere
keeps people from reading
keeps people from family
keeps people from doing active things
TVs cost a lot
informs
escape
entertainment
ads make people want things

To group her ideas, she looked for ideas that were related. She knew she had listed both good and bad effects, so she circled all the ideas that were good effects and labeled them. Then she did the same for the bad effects. The labels helped her remember what each group had in common. After sorting out her effects, she realized that one idea was not an effect at all—TVs cost a lot. So she crossed that idea off her list. Her grouped ideas are on the next page.

The groups of ideas looked like this:

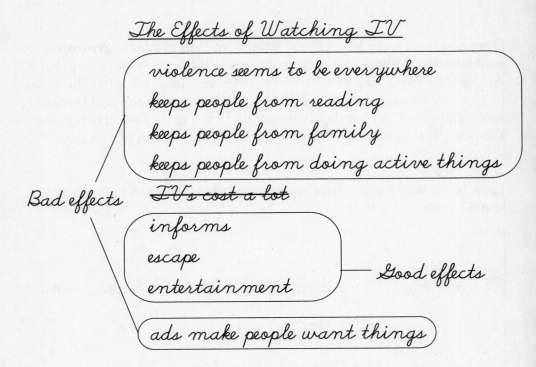

The Effects of Watching TV

violence seems to be everywhere
keeps people from reading
keeps people from family
keeps people from doing active things

Bad effects ~~TVs cost a lot~~

informs
escape
entertainment — Good effects

ads make people want things

Try to make three groups of ideas. Having three groups will help ensure enough support for your main idea.

If you have divided your list into two groups, see if one of those groups can become two smaller groups of related ideas.

It is usually not difficult to divide your list of ideas into two groups. However, since you want to write a five-paragraph essay, it is best to have three groups of related ideas for the three supporting paragraphs you will write. If you divide your largest group into two groups, each of your three groups can become a supporting paragraph for the three middle paragraphs of your essay.

To make her three groups, the writer noticed that she could make two groups from the larger group—the bad effects of TV. One group could name things that were unrealistic about TV. The other group could name things that watching TV kept people from doing.

Bad Effects

False Sense of Life

want too many
things (ads)

violence seems to
be everywhere

Keeps People from Better Things

reading

family

doing active
things

If the writer had used an idea map, many of her ideas would already be grouped and connected. She would only need to label the different groups, like this:

Ask yourself if the ideas in each group have something in common and if the labels tell how the ideas are related.

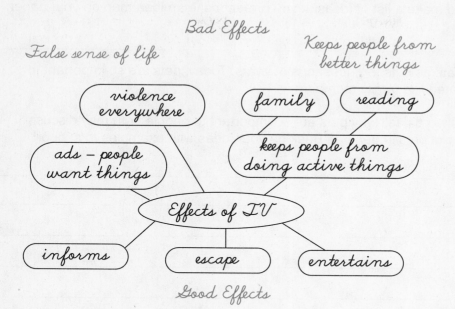

 Grouping Ideas

Read the list of ideas for the topic "What are the pros and cons of having a hobby?" Write each idea in the group where it belongs. One idea does not fit with any of the groups. Cross out that idea.

The Pros and Cons of Having a Hobby

- have fun
- can learn things
- can develop new skills
- may spend too much time away from family
- may spend too much money

- bowling is my hobby
- relieves stress
- may neglect things that need to be done
- may meet people with similar interests, make friends
- may discover a talent

Pros

Cons

Practical Reasons

Emotional and Social Reasons

_____   _____   _____

_____   _____   _____

_____   _____   _____

Organizing

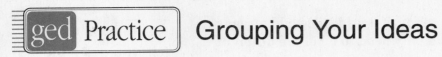

Read the writing assignment and make a list of ideas. If you prefer, make an idea map on your paper.

People have kept dogs and cats as pets for thousands of years. Today, pets are so important to their owners that they are treated like family members.

In a composition of about 200 words, tell why pets are so important to people. You may discuss the popularity of dogs, cats, or of pets in general. Back up your ideas with examples to support your point of view.

_____   _____

_____   _____

_____   _____

_____   _____

_____   _____

_____   _____

_____   _____

_____   _____

Sort your ideas into three groups of related ideas. Label the groups to show what they have in common. You may want to rewrite your lists below in three groups. If you made an idea map, label the groups.

_____   _____   _____

_____   _____   _____

_____   _____   _____

_____   _____   _____

_____   _____   _____

_____   _____   _____

_____   _____   _____

Expanding Your Groups

All your best ideas may not come to mind at once. After you've listed and grouped the first ideas you have about a topic, see if you can add more. Try using one of these methods to think of more ideas:

- Reread the topic assignment, your main idea, and the ideas you have gathered and think about them again.
- Ask yourself who, what, when, where, why, and how about the topic and see if your answers lead to more ideas. Not all the questions will apply to a topic, but most of the time, a few questions will get you started thinking.
- Think how the topic affects you and the people you know. Try to recall experiences you or people you know have had that are related to the topic.
- Try to think of things you have read or heard about the topic.

The student who wrote about the good and bad effects of watching TV did this. First, she reread the topic assignment, her main idea, and her groups. Reading her second group of bad effects—keeps people from doing other things—started her thinking about how people watch TV to avoid dealing with their problems. So, she added that idea to the group.

Next, she wanted to expand her group of good effects. To do that, she asked herself some questions.

- Who watches TV? (everyone—adults, teens, and kids)
- What kinds of shows do they watch? (adults and teens watch news, comedies, action shows, movies; young children watch educational shows and cartoons)
- How has TV affected me and the people I know? (my niece learned to count and say the alphabet from Sesame Street; a friend learned about safe dieting from TV news)

By answering her questions, she got more ideas. All three of her groups are shown with the ideas she added in color.

	Bad Effects		Good Effects
False Sense of Life	Keeps People from Better Things	information	entertainment
want too many things (ads)	reading	news programs	drawn into another world
violence seems to be everywhere	family doing active things	specials escape get lost in program	laugh and cry but not personally involved or hurt comedy shows

Expanding Groups

1. These ideas were written for the main idea "Swimming is a good sport." To expand the groups, answer the questions below. Then add your ideas to the lists.

Benefits

exercise
fun

_____

_____

_____

Little Equipment

swimming suit
towel

_____

_____

_____

Ease and Convenience

can do year round
park district pools

_____

_____

_____

- ◆ <u>Who</u> can go swimming?
- ◆ <u>What</u> do you need to go swimming?
- ◆ <u>When</u> can you go swimming?
- ◆ <u>Where</u> can you go swimming?
- ◆ <u>Why</u> do people go swimming?

2. These ideas were written for an essay on the topic "What effect would passing the GED test have on a person?" Choose one or two of the methods for discovering more ideas. Add as many ideas as you can to the groups.

Personal

feel good about yourself
learn how not to quit

_____

_____

_____

Job-related

get a more satisfying job
earn more money

_____

_____

_____

Educational

stronger reading and math
  skills
chance to go on to college

_____

_____

_____

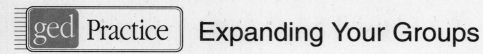

Expanding Your Groups

On page 28, you grouped ideas for the topic "Why are pets so important to people?" Use one of the methods listed on page 29 to expand your groups of ideas. You might want to work with a partner or a small group to discuss your ideas together and see how many more ideas you can include. Write down all the new ideas you come up with.

_____   _____

_____   _____

_____   _____

_____   _____

_____   _____

_____   _____

_____   _____

_____   _____

Now see if you can place all your new ideas in your groups. Do your labels still show what the ideas have in common?

_____ _____ _____

_____ _____ _____

_____ _____ _____

_____ _____ _____

_____ _____ _____

_____ _____ _____

_____ _____ _____

Organizing

Ordering Your Groups

There is one more step you should take before you write your essay. You need to decide upon a **logical order** to present your groups.

Since each of the three groups will become a paragraph in your essay, the order that you choose to present your groups is important. You want your three paragraphs ordered in a way that makes your essay strong and convincing. So you should decide which group to write about first, second, and third.

There are several ways to order ideas. For the GED essay test, there are two useful methods to learn. They are **order of importance** and **compare and contrast.**

Order of Importance

You can rank your groups of ideas from least important to most important and write about them in that order. Because this kind of organization builds from the weakest to the strongest ideas, the last thing a reader sees and what sticks in a reader's mind is the most important point.

The order of the paragraphs below is from least important to most important. As you read the paragraphs, notice the words in color. They help you understand the order of ideas.

> **tip**
>
> These words signal that ideas are organized in order of importance: *more important, most important, better, best.*

> Seat belt laws are a source of money for cities. People ticketed for not wearing seat belts must pay fines, and this money can be used to improve traffic safety.
>
> Even more important, seat belt laws themselves improve traffic safety. Just by buckling up, people are reminded to drive more safely.
>
> But the most important reason that seat belt laws are wise is that they save lives. Countless numbers of people are alive today because they were wearing their seat belts when they had an accident. Countless more have been saved from serious injury.

The writer placed his reasons for supporting seat belt laws in order from least important to most important. The most important idea, saving lives, is the last one to be read. It leaves the reader with the strongest impression.

Compare and Contrast

When you **compare** things, you show how they are alike. When you **contrast** things, you show how they are different. A GED writing assignment may ask you to compare and contrast two things, such as the problems of the past and those we encounter today. Or it may ask you to contrast different sides of a topic, such as the advantages and disadvantages of pay TV.

Contrasting is the way the student organized her essay about the good and bad effects of watching TV.

> There's no doubt that watching television can have positive effects. Adults can keep informed about current events by watching the evening news. They may even gain some practical knowledge about their health and other personal concerns. Children can learn from educational shows like Sesame Street. In addition, everyone can be entertained and even escape a little with the cartoons, comedies, movies, and action shows.
>
> **On the other hand**, watching television has some definite negative effects. Instead of just using it as a temporary escape, some people may watch television rather than deal with their problems. TV also keeps people from spending time with their family or from reading. In fact, it turns some people into couch potatoes keeping them from any physical activity.
>
> **In addition**, television gives people a false sense of what life is like. They see commercials on TV and feel they must have what's being advertised. They see violence on shows and think modern life is more violent than it really is, or they may even think it's all right to act violently.

By contrasting the negative with the positive effects of watching television, the student got her main idea across effectively. She used her first paragraph to discuss the good effects. She used her second paragraph to discuss some of the bad effects signaling this contrast with the words on the other hand. She used her third paragraph to discuss more negative effects.

These words signal that ideas are being compared: _both, also, similarly, like_. These words signal that ideas are contrasted: _on the other hand, in contrast, however, but, whereas, while_.

≣ Which Organization Should You Use?

The order you choose to present your ideas should lend the greatest support for your main idea. This chart can help you decide.

If you are writing about:	Try using:
◆ reasons or causes ◆ the qualities of one thing ◆ how you feel about an issue	◆ order of importance
◆ good and bad effects ◆ advantages and disadvantages	◆ contrast
◆ the qualities of two things	◆ compare and contrast

Before you decide how to order groups for an essay, write your main idea at the top of your paper. It can help you determine the best way to support your main idea.

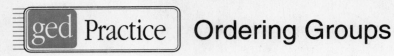

Here are some groups of ideas for two essays. Determine the order that would lend the most support to the main idea. Use the boxes to number the groups in that order.

1. **Essay topic**: Describe the advantages of swimming.

   Main idea: Swimming is a good sport.

   ☐   ☐   ☐

   Benefits

   ◆ healthy exercise
   ◆ little stress on body
   ◆ fun
   ◆ mental relaxation

   Little Equipment

   ◆ swimming suit
   ◆ towel
   ◆ maybe swimming cap

   Ease and Convenience

   ◆ can do year round
   ◆ park district pools
   ◆ beach in summer
   ◆ easy to learn

2. **Essay topic**: What effect would passing the GED test have on a person?

   Main idea: _____

   ☐   ☐   ☐

   Personal Reasons

   ◆ feel good about yourself
   ◆ learn how not to quit
   ◆ more confidence

   Job-related Reasons

   ◆ get a more satisfying job
   ◆ earn more money
   ◆ better chance for promotion

   Educational Reasons

   ◆ stronger reading and math skills
   ◆ chance to go on to college
   ◆ develop writing skills

3. Review the groups of ideas you wrote for the essay topic "Why are pets so important to people?" on pages 28 and 31. Decide on the best order and number the groups in the order you would write about them.

Here is the GED essay question you gathered ideas for in the GED Review on page 23.

Over the past few years, many people who were living in the country have moved to the city. At the same time, many people in the city have moved to the country.

In a composition of about 200 words, state whether you think life is better in the country or in the city. Give specific examples to support your view.

Use the list of ideas or idea map you made on page 23 for these exercises.

A. Group your ideas. Make three groups of related ideas with labels. You can circle and label the groups on your list or map, or you may rewrite your ideas in groups in the space below.

_____

_____

_____

_____

_____

_____

_____

_____

_____

_____

_____

_____

_____

_____

_____

B. Expand your groups. Try to add at least one idea to one or more of the groups.

C. Think about the best way to order the groups to support your main idea. Number the groups to show the order you chose.

Unit 3 WRITING

 Planning Your Essay

 Organizing Your Essay

 Writing Your Essay

- ◆ **Writing Your Introductory Paragraph**
- ◆ **Writing Your Body Paragraphs**
- ◆ **Developing Your Body Paragraphs**
- ◆ **Writing Your Concluding Paragraph**

Evaluating Your Essay

 Revising Your Essay

The third step in the POWER writing process is writing your essay. In this unit, you will learn how to use your groups of ideas to write an introductory paragraph, three well-developed body paragraphs, and a concluding paragraph. Using this approach, you will be able to produce an effective five-paragraph essay.

The Three Parts of an Essay

An essay has three basic parts. The parts follow an order, and each part has a specific purpose. In a five-paragraph essay, each part also consists of a specific number of paragraphs. Look at this plan for a five-paragraph essay.

Introduction
- consists of one paragraph
- includes the essay topic
- tells the main idea

Body
- consists of three paragraphs
- develops the topic
- supports the main idea

Conclusion
- consists of one paragraph
- sums up and reviews information in the body

To write a five-paragraph essay, one student read the following topic assignment and then completed the first two POWER steps. Read the topic and look at the student's work.

Doctors and other health experts stress the importance of exercise for good health. Over the past twenty years, many people have begun exercising regularly, yet many others still do not.

In a composition of about 200 words, discuss the importance of regular exercise. Be specific and give examples to support your opinion.

Main idea: *Regular exercise is important.*

Better Health	*Look Better*	*Feel Better*
stronger heart	*lose weight*	*feel good about*
breathe better	*firm muscles*	*how you look*
more endurance	*healthier skin*	*more self-esteem*
burns calories	*and hair*	*reduces tension*
		feel more relaxed

Then the student wrote the following essay. Read it and notice how the three parts of an essay are contained in the five paragraphs.

Introduction

Many people exercise regularly, yet many others do not. If those who don't exercise knew how important it is, they would all start exercise programs. Regular exercise makes and keeps you fit. In fact, it helps you look and feel fit in addition to being fit.

Body

First of all, regular exercise is good for your health. When you run, bicycle, or do some other aerobic activity three times a week, your heart becomes stronger, and your breathing improves. These physical changes increase your endurance. You actually feel like you have more energy. In addition, muscles that are working burn more fat calories.

Exercise can help improve not only your health but also your looks. Because your body burns more calories, you lose weight and look slimmer and trimmer. Your muscles become firm. You seem more youthful and energetic. In addition, better circulation gives your skin and hair a healthy glow.

Perhaps all these physical benefits lead Body to the most important result of regular exercise—it makes you feel better. Exercise reduces tension in your muscles and makes you more relaxed. You feel rested and ready to go during the day, and you sleep better at night. Because you look better, you also just naturally feel better about your body and about yourself. Your self-esteem increases.

With all these benefits of regular Conclusion exercise, it's hard to understand why someone would not work out. If you exercise regularly, your body and your mind will appreciate it.

Paragraphs and Topic Sentences

Before you write your essay, you need to know how to develop a good paragraph. To do so, focus on the groups of ideas you wrote in POWER Step 2. Each group of ideas will become a paragraph in your essay.

Each paragraph will have a **topic sentence** that tells the main idea of the paragraph. The other ideas become the **supporting details** of the paragraph. You can write the topic sentence at the beginning, middle, or end of a paragraph. A paragraph may be written in these three ways:

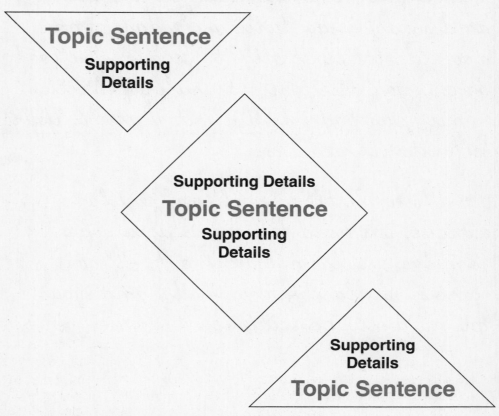

Read this paragraph. Where is the topic sentence?

> The cost of living has risen steadily over the past several decades. While a loaf of bread cost 30 cents 30 years ago, today it can cost 5 or 6 times that. Just 25 years ago, you could purchase a new car for about $4,000. Today the average cost of a new car is closer to $14,000. The price of housing is another example of rising costs. In the 1960s, an apartment rented for as little as $125 a month. With today's rents, that same apartment would cost at least $500 per month.

The first sentence of the paragraph is the topic sentence. It tells the main idea of the paragraph. The rest of the sentences support the paragraph's main idea with details that contrast the prices of bread, cars, and housing.

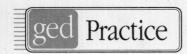

Read each paragraph. Then answer the questions.

1. A good worker is someone who understands how important it is not to be absent too often and who gets the job done. People seldom get fired because the quality of their work is poor. Instead, more people lose their jobs for such things as not showing up for work or not doing their job. Managers need to know that they can count on their workers to be on the job. Employers have little tolerance for workers who talk so much with their coworkers that they can't finish a job.

    a. What is the paragraph about? _____

    _____

    b. Underline the topic sentence.

    c. List some supporting details. _____

    _____

    _____

    _____

    _____

2. Over the years people have moved into much of the wilderness area where bald eagles live. Eagles build their nests in the tops of tall trees near water. More and more of that land has become farmland or city streets. And the pollution of lakes and rivers has poisoned the fish that eagles eat. As a result, the bald eagles have had problems reproducing. They lay eggs that don't hatch. In addition, until 1950 hunters and trappers were allowed to kill many bald eagles. It is ironic that Americans are directly responsible for making the bald eagle, their national bird, an endangered species.

    a. What is the paragraph about? _____

    _____

    b. Underline the topic sentence.

    c. List some supporting details. _____

    _____

    _____

    _____

    _____

The paragraphs below have supporting details but no topic sentences. Three choices for a topic sentence follow each paragraph. Circle the letter of the best topic sentence for each paragraph.

1.   Some companies put coupons or rebate offers in newspapers or send them through the mail. Other companies place coupons or rebate offers right on the packaging. The companies hope consumers will buy their products because of these offers. The value of a coupon is subtracted from the cost of the item when it is purchased. To get a rebate, a consumer must send a receipt and a product label to the company and wait for a rebate check in the mail. Shoppers can save money by taking advantage of these manufacturer incentives.

   a. Consumers can make ends meet by buying generic brands and taking advantage of coupon offers.

   b. Many manufacturers try to increase sales by offering money-saving coupons or rebates.

   c. Manufacturers should lower the cost of their products rather than use coupons to get shoppers to buy their products.

2.   In a crime-stoppers program, someone may be paid for supplying information that leads to the arrest and conviction of a person who commits a felony. The identity of the person who reports information is kept secret so that no harm will come to him or her. Funds to support this crime-stoppers program come from tax dollars as well as private contributions. This effort has assisted many communities in solving criminal cases.

   a. An organization will reward people who report information about crimes that have been committed.

   b. Crime is increasing in this country at an alarming rate, and something has to be done about it.

   c. There is a better way to fight crime than relying on taxpayers' dollars.

3.   Even before you have an interview, your résumé may give a prospective employer a first impression of you. An employer may screen out an applicant with a résumé that makes a bad impression. A résumé should be neatly typed and easy to read. It should also be complete enough to tell important information about you. If it is organized well, it can be thorough without being too long; one page is preferred. You can use underlining, capital letters, and asterisks to point out important information you would like an employer to know.

   a. A résumé is a tool that can help you get a job interview.

   b. When you have an interview for a job, you should tell about all your past work experience.

   c. Even if you have a great résumé, you won't get the job if you arrive late for an interview.

Write a topic sentence for each paragraph.

1.   Two hundred years ago, few people could read or write. At that time, people could get jobs and make a living without having to read or to write their names. However, over the years, jobs have become more complex and complicated. Machinery has replaced workers that performed manual labor. The ability to think has become much more important. Jobs that require workers to read, write, compute, and think have become the norm.

_____

_____

2.   Smoking cigarettes is bad for your health. In fact, tobacco use in any form has been proven harmful. Thousands of people die each year from lung cancer, and thousands more die from heart disease that is linked to smoking. In addition, smoking is an expensive habit. Heavy smokers may spend as much as $7 per day on cigarettes. That adds up to about $210 a month! Think of all the things a person could buy with that money.

_____

_____

3.   There are consumer groups you may go to for financial help. They will review your finances and advise you on how to reduce your debt. They will help you make a budget to pay your creditors. They will even tell you if your financial situation is so complicated that you need to see an attorney. People to whom you owe money will often work with you as well. They may be willing to reduce your monthly payments so that you can afford to pay them. Most important, you can learn to live within your means.

_____

_____

4.   Pharmacists do not generally mark a prescription drug with an expiration date, although the container usually shows the date of the prescription. Generally, if the drug is more than one year old, it should not be taken. A good rule to remember about the length of time to keep prescription drugs is, "When in doubt, throw it out."

_____

_____

Writing Your Introductory Paragraph

A good introductory paragraph does several things:

- ◆ It states the topic of the essay.
- ◆ It tells your reader what your main idea is.
- ◆ It gives your reader a preview of your essay.
- ◆ It provides your reader with background information.

Sometimes your main idea becomes clearer after you've planned your essay. Your thesis statement can pinpoint exactly what you want to say.

The topic of an essay is stated in a sentence called the **thesis statement.** You can write the thesis statement by rewriting the main idea (POWER Step 1). Expand the main idea by adding words or phrases that help explain or strengthen the statement. Read this example that shows how a student expanded a main idea into a thesis statement.

Main idea: Comedies are my favorite TV shows.

Thesis statement: I like comedy shows more than anything else on TV.

For a good introductory paragraph, you will also need to write one or more **preview sentences.** Preview sentences tell your reader what to expect in the essay. To write preview sentences, use your labeled groups (POWER Step 2) and tell about them in a way that might interest a reader. The ideas you present in preview sentences should be brief and general.

You can use the background information in the topic assignment to write background sentences.

Finally, you can add **background sentences**—one or two sentences that give general information about the topic. Background sentences are not necessary, but they can help introduce your reader to the topic.

Here is the introductory paragraph from the essay on pages 38–39. In the planning stage, the main idea was, "Regular exercise is important." After thinking about his ideas, the writer expanded the main idea and wrote a thesis statement. He included background information, and he wrote a preview sentence that told what his essay would be about.

Many people exercise regularly, yet many others do not. If those who don't exercise knew how important it is, they would all start exercise programs. — Background Sentences

Regular exercise makes and keeps you fit. — Thesis Statement

In fact, it helps you look and feel fit in addition to being fit. — Preview Sentence

Write introductory paragraphs for the topic assignments. Follow these steps.

a. Read each topic assignment. On your paper, use POWER Steps 1 and 2 to write a main idea, create groups of ideas, and label them. Topic 1 has been done for you. Use it as a model.

b. Then write an introductory paragraph for each essay.

TOPIC 1

Professional athletes today earn salaries in excess of $100,000 a year. Some people believe these athletes deserve the money they make, while others think athletes are paid too much.

Write an essay of 200 words discussing the high salaries of professional athletes. You may agree or disagree that salaries are too high. Be specific and use examples to support your view.

Main idea: Athletes earn their money.

Physical Work
- requires intense work
- can be hurt or hospitalized
- chance of long-term injury
- lots of effort during game

Professionals
- train for a long time
- work hard to become pro
- have to stay on a strict diet
- have no privacy

Serve the Community
- act as positive role models
- do commercials against drugs
- work for charities

TOPIC 2

Many people claim that rock music is a bad influence on young people. They feel it encourages drug use and inappropriate behavior. Others believe that rock music is good entertainment. They don't think that it causes social problems.

In an essay of 200 words, discuss the influence of rock music on young people. You may discuss positive or negative influences, or both. Be specific and use examples to support your view.

TOPIC 3

How to be a good parent has become a popular topic. Magazines and books offer parenting advice, classes teach parents how to raise children, and TV shows present parenting experts.

In a composition of about 200 words, discuss the role of being a parent. You may discuss the responsibilities, the pleasures, or both. Support your view with details and examples.

Writing the Body Paragraphs

Now you're ready to write the **body paragraphs** of your essay. The three body paragraphs develop your topic. They back up the thesis statement in your introductory paragraph with supporting ideas.

To write three body paragraphs, use your expanded groups of ideas (POWER Step 2). Use the labels you gave to each group to help you write topic sentences for the paragraphs. The topic sentences should tell the main ideas of the paragraphs.

Then use the ideas from each group to write supporting sentences for the paragraphs. To be sure your supporting sentences stay on the topic, keep your lists handy as you write. And remember to follow the order you chose for the paragraphs (POWER Step 2).

Here are the body paragraphs from the essay about exercise on pages 38–39. Compare the paragraphs with the three groups of ideas.

> **tip**
>
> **You can place a topic sentence at the beginning, middle, or end of a paragraph, but it's a good idea to put it first so your reader knows what the paragraph is about.**

Better Health

stronger heart
breathe better
more endurance
burns calories

Topic Sentence ⟶

First of all, regular exercise is good for your health. When you run, bicycle, or do some other aerobic activity three times a week, your heart becomes stronger, and your breathing improves. These physical changes increase your endurance. You actually feel like you have more energy. In addition, muscles that are working burn more fat calories.

Look Better

lose weight
firm muscles
healthier skin
  and hair

Topic Sentence ⟶

Exercise can help improve not only your health but also your looks. Because your body burns more calories, you lose weight and look slimmer and trimmer. Your muscles become firm. You seem more youthful and energetic. In addition, better circulation gives your skin and hair a healthy glow.

<u>*Feel Better*</u>

feel good about
 how you look
more self esteem
reduces tension
feel more relaxed

Topic Sentence ⟶

Perhaps all these physical benefits lead to the most important result of regular exercise—it makes you feel better. Exercise reduces tension in your muscles and makes you more relaxed. You feel rested and ready to go during the day, and you sleep better at night. Because you look better, you also just naturally feel better about your body and about yourself. Your self-esteem increases.

Did you notice that the writer added some details that weren't in the groups? While writing the body, new ideas occurred to him. You can use new ideas that occur to you during <u>any</u> of the POWER steps. Just be sure they support the thesis statement of the essay as well as the topic sentence of the paragraph.

 ## Writing Body Paragraphs

To practice writing body paragraphs, look back at the GED Practice on page 45. Follow these steps for each topic assignment.

a. Review the lists of ideas and the introductory paragraph you wrote.

b. Choose an order for the lists.

c. Use the labels to write topic sentences for the body paragraphs.

d. Use the ideas in each list to write supporting sentences.

e. Add details if they come to you.

1. Write three body paragraphs justifying the high salaries of professional athletes. Use the same sheet of paper that you used to write the introductory paragraph.

2. Write three body paragraphs about whether or not rock music is a bad influence on young people.

3. Write three body paragraphs about the responsibilities, pleasures, or both of being a parent.

Developing Your Body Paragraphs

As you write your GED essay, don't worry about making mistakes in spelling, punctuation, or grammar. You can correct them after you get your ideas down.

For the body of an essay, you write about the ideas you thought of and organized. To write a strong essay, you want to develop those ideas. **Developing** means explaining by giving details and examples.

When you develop the ideas in a body paragraph, you support the main idea of the paragraph's topic sentence. When you support the topic sentences of all your body paragraphs, you are supporting the thesis statement for your entire essay. In that way, you write a strong, effective essay.

As you write your body paragraphs, try to add enough **details** to explain and support your ideas. Look at how one writer added support to the original ideas on the importance of regular exercise. The writer added more detailed information to explain the idea.

Supporting Idea	Detail in Body Paragraph
◆ burns calories *was explained as*	◆ muscles that are working burn more fat calories
◆ lose weight *was explained as*	◆ you lose weight and look slimmer and trimmer

Another way to help develop a topic is to add **examples**. An example names a person or explains a situation that helps illustrate what you mean. Read these examples that the writer added to the essay on exercise to illustrate the idea.

Supporting Idea	Example in Body Paragraph
◆ regular exercise *was illustrated with*	◆ running, bicycling, or some other aerobic activity three times a week
◆ feel more relaxed *was illustrated with*	◆ you feel rested and ready to go during the day, and you sleep better at night

Rewrite each statement below by adding more details to the supporting idea. If you want help thinking of details, use the questions that follow.

1. Chocolate tastes good. (How does it smell? How does it feel in your mouth? How does it make you feel when you eat it? What does it taste better than?)

_____

_____

_____

2. Sleep is important. (Why is it important? How does it make you feel? What does lack of sleep do to you? What happens when you sleep?)

_____

_____

_____

Add one or more examples to each statement below. If you want help thinking of examples, use the questions that follow.

3. Our lives are filled with noise. (What makes the noises? What kinds of noises are involved? Who makes each noise?)

For example, _____

_____

_____

4. People are sometimes rude. (Who is sometimes rude? How are people rude? What do they do that is rude?)

For example, _____

_____

_____

Choose one of the topics on page 47—athletes' salaries, rock music, or parenting. Add additional details and examples to develop the paragraphs you wrote. Ask yourself questions to help you think of additional details and examples. Add them in the margins or rewrite the paragraphs.

The Concluding Paragraph

The last paragraph of your essay is the **concluding paragraph.** It gives the same information that the introductory paragraph gives, but it is written from a different perspective. Instead of previewing your essay, the concluding paragraph looks back at the ideas in your essay. This final paragraph restates your topic and reviews your ideas.

Reread the concluding paragraph from the essay about exercise.

As you write your essay, you may want to add or change phrases or sentences. Leave wide margins so that you can make changes easily.

With all these benefits of regular exercise, it's hard to understand why someone would not work out. If you exercise regularly, your body and your mind will appreciate it.

You can see that the concluding paragraph restates the topic and reviews the supporting details. It includes some advice and ends with a strong statement about what will happen when the advice is followed.

 The Concluding Paragraph

Reread the introductory and body paragraphs you wrote for practice on pages 45 and 47. Write a concluding paragraph for each essay.

1. Write a concluding paragraph for the essay justifying the high salaries of professional athletes.

_____

_____

_____

_____

_____

_____

_____

2. Write a concluding paragraph for the essay about whether rock music is a bad influence on young people.

_____

_____

_____

_____

_____

_____

_____

3. Write a concluding paragraph for the essay about the responsibilities, the pleasures, or both of being a parent.

_____

_____

_____

_____

_____

_____

_____

_____

Here is the topic assignment you organized ideas for in the GED Review on page 35.

> Over the past few years, many people who were living in the country have moved to the city. At the same time, many people in the city have moved to the country.
>
> In a composition of about 200 words, state whether you think life is better in the country or in the city. Give specific examples to support your view.

Use the ordered groups of ideas you made for these exercises. Write paragraphs on the lines that follow or use a copy of the answer sheet on pages 156–157.

1. Write an introductory paragraph. Use your main idea sentence to write a thesis statement. Use the labels of the idea groups to write one or more preview sentences. If you want to write background sentences, use the background information from the topic assignment.

2. Write three body paragraphs. Use the labels of the idea groups to write the topic sentences. Use the ideas in each group to write supporting sentences. Develop each paragraph with details and examples. Write the paragraphs in the order you selected on page 35.

3. Write a concluding paragraph. Restate your topic and review your ideas.

_____

_____

_____

_____

_____

_____

_____

_____

_____

_____

_____

_____

Planning Your Essay

Organizing Your Essay

Writing Your Essay

Evaluating Your Essay

Revising Your Essay

- ◆ **Evaluating Your Ideas and Organization**
- ◆ **Evaluating Your Use of the Conventions of English**

The fourth step in the POWER writing process is evaluation. In this unit, you'll learn how a GED test scorer will evaluate and score your essay. Then you'll learn how to evaluate both the overall presentation of your ideas and your use of punctuation, grammar, and other conventions of English to improve your essay.

Holistic Scoring

GED test scorers will evaluate your essay **holistically**—by judging its overall effectiveness. To the scorers, how clearly you present your thesis statement and how well you support it are the most important things they judge. A few misspelled words or a few errors in grammar will not cause your essay to receive a low score although too many errors might. The GED Essay Scoring Guide that follows tells what characteristics the essay scorers look for when they read an essay.

GED Essay Scoring Guide

Copyright © 1987, GED Testing Service

Papers will show *some or all* of the following characteristics.

Upper-half papers have a clear, definite purpose pursued with varying degrees of effectiveness. They have a structure that shows evidence of some deliberate planning. The writer's control of the conventions of Standard Written English (spelling, punctuation, grammar, word choice, and sentence structure) ranges from fairly reliable at 4 to confident and accomplished at 6.

6   The *6 paper* offers sophisticated ideas within an organizational framework that is clear and appropriate for the topic. The supporting statements are particularly effective because of their substance, specificity, or illustrative quality. The writing is vivid and precise, although it may contain an occasional error in the conventions of Standard Written English.

5   The *5 paper* is clearly organized with effective support for each of the writer's major points. While the writing offers substantive ideas, it lacks the fluency found in the 6 paper. Although there are some errors, the conventions of Standard Written English are consistently under control.

4   The *4 paper* shows evidence of the writer's organizational plan. Support, though adequate, tends to be less extensive or effective than that found in the 5 paper. The writer generally observes the conventions of Standard Written English. The errors that are present are not severe enough to interfere significantly with the writer's main purpose.

Lower-half papers either fail to convey a purpose sufficiently or lack one entirely. Consequently, their structure ranges from rudimentary at 3, to random at 2, to absent at 1. Control of the conventions of Standard Written English tends to follow this same gradient.

3   The *3 paper* usually shows some evidence of planning, although the development is insufficient. The supporting statements may be limited to a listing or a repetition of ideas. The 3 paper often demonstrates repeated weaknesses in the conventions of Standard Written English.

2   The *2 paper* is characterized by a marked lack of organization or inadequate support for ideas. The development is usually superficial or unfocused. Errors in the conventions of Standard Written English may seriously interfere with the overall effectiveness of this paper.

1   The *1 paper* lacks purpose or development. The dominant feature is the absence of control of structure or the conventions of Standard Written English. The deficiencies are so severe that the writer's ideas are difficult or impossible to understand.

*   An asterisk code is reserved for papers that are blank, illegible, or written on a topic other than the one assigned. Because these papers cannot be scored, a Writing Skills Test composite score cannot be reported.

Here and on page 57 is an example of an essay and the score it received. Read the writing assignment and the essay. Then look over the explanation of the essay's score.

Over the past few years, many people who were living in the country have moved to the city. At the same time, many people in the city have moved to the country.

In a composition of about 200 words, state whether you think life is better in the country or in the city. Give specific examples to support your view.

Life in the big city, and life in a small town vary sharply. There are advantages as well as disadvantages to life in the city, just as there are good and bad things about small towns.

Some of the bad points to city life are high crime, over crowded housing, and heavy traffic. Life can also be very rewarding in the city, as there are more places of employment as well as intertainment.

Life in a small town moves at a slower rate. The people are friendlier, because of a lower crime rate. The housing is spaced more openly, and the highways are not as crowded, because there are less intertainment and employment oppurtunities.

In my oppinion life in the small town far out weighs life in the city because life at a slower pace is more rewarding.

The essay received a score of 3. It has good organization, but the topic and supporting ideas need more development; details in the body paragraphs are repetitious. There are also some errors in the conventions of English—mainly in spelling.

Evaluating an Essay

GED scorers read an essay once and then assign a score to it. However, when you evaluate your essay, you want to read it more carefully to see how to improve it and get a higher score. There are four areas to consider when evaluating your essay—**organization, support, clarity,** and **conventions of English.** You can use this check list to help you.

Yes No
Organization
☐ ☐ (1) Does the introductory paragraph include the essay topic and a thesis statement?
☐ ☐ (2) Does each body paragraph have a topic sentence and details related to the topic sentence?
☐ ☐ (3) Does the concluding paragraph restate the topic and review the ideas?
☐ ☐ (4) Does the essay stick to the topic?

Support
☐ ☐ (5) Do the paragraphs include specific details and examples that support the topic sentences?
☐ ☐ (6) Does the essay support the thesis statement?

Clarity
☐ ☐ (7) Is the main idea understandable?
☐ ☐ (8) Are the supporting ideas expressed clearly?

Conventions of English
☐ ☐ (9) Are the ideas written in complete sentences?
☐ ☐ (10) Is the grammar correct?
☐ ☐ (11) Are punctuation marks used correctly?
☐ ☐ (12) Are words spelled correctly?
☐ ☐ (13) Are capital letters used correctly?

To evaluate your essay, read it twice. During the first reading, concentrate on the first three areas of the check list—organization, support, and clarity. These questions help you evaluate your presentation of ideas. During the second reading, concentrate on the last area of the check list, the conventions of English.

When you evaluate your GED essay, read it carefully but not too slowly. If you read slowly, you may pay too much attention to minor details instead of your presentation of ideas.

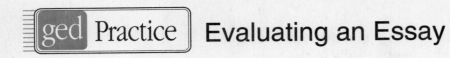

The six essays on this page and the following pages were written for the writing assignment on page 56, city living versus country living. Work independently or with a partner to evaluate the essays. Use these steps to evaluate them.

1. Read each essay once to evaluate it as a GED scorer would. Use the GED scoring guidelines on page 55 to assign a score of * to 6.

2. Evaluate each essay again to improve the presentation of ideas. Answer the questions in the first three areas of the check list.

3. Check over the essay a third time to evaluate the control of the conventions of English. Answer the questions in the last area of the check list.

Essay 1

I think that rural life is better than urban. Because you save time and money. You don't have to go to the grocery store as much. You don't have to commute back & forth on a bus. You can do your washing on hand. It is less complicated. The crime rate is very low. Less traffic. Don't worry that much about being mugged or robbed because the town is so small. The people within the community. They seem very nice. The atmosphere smells very clean.

Essay 1

○   ○   ○   ○   ○   ○   ○

*   1   2   3   4   5   6

Yes **No**

Organization

☐ ☐ (1) Does the introductory paragraph include the essay topic and a thesis statement?

☐ ☐ (2) Does each body paragraph have a topic sentence and details related to the topic sentence?

☐ ☐ (3) Does the concluding paragraph restate the topic and review the ideas?

☐ ☐ (4) Does the essay stick to the topic?

Support

☐ ☐ (5) Do the paragraphs include specific details and examples that support the topic sentences?

☐ ☐ (6) Does the essay support the thesis statement?

Clarity

☐ ☐ (7) Is the main idea understandable?

☐ ☐ (8) Are the supporting ideas expressed clearly?

Conventions of English

☐ ☐ (9) Are the ideas written in complete sentences?

☐ ☐ (10) Is the grammar correct?

☐ ☐ (11) Are punctuation marks used correctly?

☐ ☐ (12) Are words spelled correctly?

☐ ☐ (13) Are capital letters used correctly?

Essay 2

City Dwells, for year's and year's this city founders have started to move from the complicated population and noice cities of America to slower and busyless life in small towns. the citizens make a very good decitions for heathy life and tranquility on rural town in to big forest filled with beatiful bird songs and quiet nights. Out from the cars noice and smoked factorys with trash on the streets accidents on the roads, crimes bad situations with frenetized people and dark skys poluted with gases poisining the city trees and litte birds destroy human life slowly but efectivily like some to hardful venom contaminaded lakes and parks with chemicals and drug's. Drug's! the most dengerous numer one problem on the big's city can destroy families and poisoning the young's and the oldest to! but move to small town have little problems for the comfort and comodity on restaurants theaters and quikly movement to one place to other but with this little diference the small town's is the big diference to the big troubles on the populed city.
Welcome to the forest.

Essay 2

○   ○   ○   ○   ○   ○   ○
*   1   2   3   4   5   6

Yes   No
□   □   **Organization**
            (1) Does the introductory paragraph include the essay topic and a thesis statement?
□   □   (2) Does each body paragraph have a topic sentence and details related to the topic sentence?
□   □   (3) Does the concluding paragraph restate the topic and review the ideas?
□   □   (4) Does the essay stick to the topic?

                Support
□   □   (5) Do the paragraphs include specific details and examples that support the topic sentences?
□   □   (6) Does the essay support the thesis statement?

                Clarity
□   □   (7) Is the main idea understandable?
□   □   (8) Are the supporting ideas expressed clearly?

            Conventions of English
□   □   (9) Are the ideas written in complete sentences?
□   □   (10) Is the grammar correct?
□   □   (11) Are punctuation marks used correctly?
□   □   (12) Are words spelled correctly?
□   □   (13) Are capital letters used correctly?

Persons living in the city have certain advantiges over persons living in small towns.

Persons starting their own companies, almost always do better in the big city rather than starting componies in small town. For example, population is greater there is more demand, more demand means a stonger company This also makes it a little easier on the unemployed a stronger company needs more workers.

Also persons living in the city have good times by going out dancing and eating at fancy places, going bowling, seeing movies at the cinema, driving the town and meeting other people and maybe meeting other friends, just plain having a good time.

Persons living in small towns have a simple and good life because thats where they have always lived and made a fair living, but cities all over the United States will always do better than small towns because the more power, and money and activities for the residents better the recovery in hard times.

Essay 3

○	○	○	○	○	○	○
*	1	2	3	4	5	6

Yes No

Organization

☐ ☐ (1) Does the introductory paragraph include the essay topic and a thesis statement?

☐ ☐ (2) Does each body paragraph have a topic sentence and details related to the topic sentence?

☐ ☐ (3) Does the concluding paragraph restate the topic and review the ideas?

☐ ☐ (4) Does the essay stick to the topic?

Support

☐ ☐ (5) Do the paragraphs include specific details and examples that support the topic sentences?

☐ ☐ (6) Does the essay support the thesis statement?

Clarity

☐ ☐ (7) Is the main idea understandable?

☐ ☐ (8) Are the supporting ideas expressed clearly?

Conventions of English

☐ ☐ (9) Are the ideas written in complete sentences?

☐ ☐ (10) Is the grammar correct?

☐ ☐ (11) Are punctuation marks used correctly?

☐ ☐ (12) Are words spelled correctly?

☐ ☐ (13) Are capital letters used correctly?

In spite of the obvious advantages of big city life, I'll take the small town everytime. Life in a small town is superior because of the quality of the [~~your~~] relationships you can develop and because small town life is less stressful.

The quality of the relationships one can develop in a small town are far better than those that you have in a large, faceless city. People in small towns [can] really get to know one another. They help each other out and share in each others successes. [They have time for one another.] People in small towns don't have to fear strangers and can trust others. They can count on there being someone there for them even if they are new to town or have no family close by. People in small towns [tend] [~~have the time~~] to express their affection for each other. [They are more open and giving.] It is easier to [get to] know and be known by people in a small rural setting.

In addition [the] lifestyle in a small town [is] [~~has~~] much less stressful than that of a large city. [~~There~~] [People] seems to be in less of a hurry. There are no crowds to shove and pressure you. Traffic is not a daily nightmare. Crime is not so very plentiful. [Drugs don't tempt your children on every corner.] These things that create stress in the life of an urban dweller are just not present in the lives of people living in small towns.

Because relationships are easier to develop in a small town and stress is far less noticeable, life in the small town seems superior to living in a city. I'd pick the [~~the~~] rural life if I had my choice.

Essay 4

○   ○   ○   ○   ○   ○   ○
*   1   2   3   4   5   6

Yes   **No**

Organization

☐ ☐   (1) Does the introductory paragraph include the essay topic and a thesis statement?

☐ ☐   (2) Does each body paragraph have a topic sentence and details related to the topic sentence?

☐ ☐   (3) Does the concluding paragraph restate the topic and review the ideas?

☐ ☐   (4) Does the essay stick to the topic?

Support

☐ ☐   (5) Do the paragraphs include specific details and examples that support the topic sentences?

☐ ☐   (6) Does the essay support the thesis statement?

Clarity

☐ ☐   (7) Is the main idea understandable?

☐ ☐   (8) Are the supporting ideas expressed clearly?

Conventions of English

☐ ☐   (9) Are the ideas written in complete sentences?

☐ ☐   (10) Is the grammar correct?

☐ ☐   (11) Are punctuation marks used correctly?

☐ ☐   (12) Are words spelled correctly?

☐ ☐   (13) Are capital letters used correctly?

Essay 5

I prefer to live in a small town. Rural life is more relaxed and less expensive than life in a large city. The pace of life in a small town is far more relaxed than ~~life~~ living in a large city. People are not in such a hurry in a small town. They have time for one another and for the little pleasures in life. Because there are fewer people, there are shorter lines at the bank, the grocery and the post office. People don't get so tense because these everyday activities take less time than in the big city. Drivers don't get stuck in traffic and worry about being late for appointments. This little things add up to fewer hassles and a more relaxed atmosphere.

The cost of living in a big city is a disadvantage, too. ~~Rural~~ Housing in rural towns is cheaper and food cost less. Kids don't go to private schools much so education is not as much. There are fewer reasons to have to dress up and buying clothes is not so important. Keeping up with the Jones is not nearly so important. People can just be theirselves.

Living in a small town is a more relaxed and less expensive way to live. I would rather live in a small town anyday.

Essay 5

○   ○   ○   ○   ○   ○   ○
*   1   2   3   4   5   6

Yes   No

Organization

- ☐ ☐   (1) Does the introductory paragraph include the essay topic and a thesis statement?
- ☐ ☐   (2) Does each body paragraph have a topic sentence and details related to the topic sentence?
- ☐ ☐   (3) Does the concluding paragraph restate the topic and review the ideas?
- ☐ ☐   (4) Does the essay stick to the topic?

Support

- ☐ ☐   (5) Do the paragraphs include specific details and examples that support the topic sentences?
- ☐ ☐   (6) Does the essay support the thesis statement?

Clarity

- ☐ ☐   (7) Is the main idea understandable?
- ☐ ☐   (8) Are the supporting ideas expressed clearly?

Conventions of English

- ☐ ☐   (9) Are the ideas written in complete sentences?
- ☐ ☐   (10) Is the grammar correct?
- ☐ ☐   (11) Are punctuation marks used correctly?
- ☐ ☐   (12) Are words spelled correctly?
- ☐ ☐   (13) Are capital letters used correctly?

Essay 6

If one were to contemplate the advantages and disadvantages of city living versus country or small town living various aspects of both senerios should be equally eveluated, with fairness to pros and cons alike.

City living for instance has several good points, when you dwell in the city (city-dwellers) as they are called, are people surrounded by convenience, their work place their homes, schools and shopping are within the peramiters or just on the outskirts of the city itself. This lends a tremendous advantage of locality, gives an edge to the city dwellers, as everything is right there within reach, they don't have far to go to get from point 'A' to point 'B' so to speak.

On the other hand, the disadvantages are also plentiful. there are traffic jams almost constantly. Most always smog surrounds the city with an unhealthy shroud of various pollutants, many of wich are harmful to breath on certain days when it is exceptionally thick. The crime rate is higher in big urban cities, many people are in transient and just drifting through, on their way to who knows where?

Drugs are always in the picture, many big time dealers prefer the city as it gives them a wider variety of people to deal their venom to. Children get caught up in the horrible senerio, drugs and drug related problems plauge big cities. Because of all these neggitive things people are looking to smaller towns and country living to sort of get away from the overcrowding and anonaminity that city living entails. smaller towns by contrast have almost as many ammenities as their bigger more overcrowded counter-parts, people seem to interact better, there is a sense of belonging, small town folk are most always better adjusted. they have fewer problems, you might say they do have some of the problems of the bigger cities but certainly on a much smaller scale.

We as a people have to contend with whatever modes of living nessitates our survival, sometimes we have no choice in where we would prefer to live as in where we actually have to live. Jobs in the 80's often dictate our locale, a lot of times we get a job transfer taking us to various localities. military people for instance must relocate periodically. It is my feeling that one must make the best of a city or town and as a people we most always can etch out a good standard of living whereverer we live.

Essay 6

○   ○   ○   ○   ○   ○   ○
*   1   2   3   4   5   6

Yes   No

Organization

☐ ☐   (1) Does the introductory paragraph include the essay topic and a thesis statement?

☐ ☐   (2) Does each body paragraph have a topic sentence and details related to the topic sentence?

☐ ☐   (3) Does the concluding paragraph restate the topic and review the ideas?

☐ ☐   (4) Does the essay stick to the topic?

Support

☐ ☐   (5) Do the paragraphs include specific details and examples that support the topic sentences?

☐ ☐   (6) Does the essay support the thesis statement?

Clarity

☐ ☐   (7) Is the main idea understandable?

☐ ☐   (8) Are the supporting ideas expressed clearly?

Conventions of English

☐ ☐   (9) Are the ideas written in complete sentences?

☐ ☐   (10) Is the grammar correct?

☐ ☐   (11) Are punctuation marks used correctly?

☐ ☐   (12) Are words spelled correctly?

☐ ☐   (13) Are capital letters used correctly?

Turn back to the essay you wrote on pages 52–53 about whether life is better in the country or the city.

Evaluate your essay using this check list.

When you write your GED essay, don't take time to score it. Spend about five minutes evaluating it with the check list in mind and decide how you can improve it.

Yes	No	**Organization**
☐	☐	(1) Does the introductory paragraph include the essay topic and a thesis statement?
☐	☐	(2) Does each body paragraph have a topic sentence and details related to the topic sentence?
☐	☐	(3) Does the concluding paragraph restate the topic and review the ideas?
☐	☐	(4) Does the essay stick to the topic?

Support

☐	☐	(5) Do the paragraphs include specific details and examples that support the topic sentences?
☐	☐	(6) Does the essay support the thesis statement?

Clarity

☐	☐	(7) Is the main idea understandable?
☐	☐	(8) Are the supporting ideas expressed clearly?

Conventions of English

☐	☐	(9) Are the ideas written in complete sentences?
☐	☐	(10) Is the grammar correct?
☐	☐	(11) Are punctuation marks used correctly?
☐	☐	(12) Are words spelled correctly?
☐	☐	(13) Are capital letters used correctly?

Planning Your Essay

Organizing Your Essay

Writing Your Essay

Evaluating Your Essay

Revising Your Essay

♦ **Revising Your Ideas and Organization**

♦ **Revising Your Use of the Conventions of English**

The fifth step in the POWER writing process is revising. Revising an essay means changing the parts you think are weak. In this unit, you will learn to use the evaluation of your essay (POWER Step 4) to revise the presentation of ideas and correct any mistakes. The result will be a stronger, more effective essay.

A Two-Step Process

When you evaluate an essay (POWER Step 4), you identify areas that need strengthening or correcting. To revise the essay, decide how to change those areas and then make the changes.

Because evaluation is a two-step process, it's best to revise in two steps, too. First, evaluate and revise your ideas and organization. Then evaluate and revise your use of the conventions of English. This second step of revision is sometimes called **proofreading.**

When you revise, you don't need to rewrite your essay. Instead, you can use these revision methods:
- ◆ Cross out any unwanted words or phrases.
- ◆ Make corrections or add ideas between the lines or in the margin.
- ◆ Use a caret (^) to show where additions belong.
- ◆ Rewrite any part that is illegible or too messy to read.

Revision is a two-step process:
STEP 1: Read your essay to evaluate the ideas and the organization. If necessary, revise them.
STEP 2: Proofread your essay for your use of the conventions of English. Then make necessary corrections.

Revising Your Ideas and Organization

When you evaluated your presentation of ideas (POWER Step 4), you asked yourself three groups of questions:

Yes No
Organization
- ☐ ☐ (1) Does the introductory paragraph include the essay topic and a thesis statement?
- ☐ ☐ (2) Does each body paragraph have a topic sentence and details related to the topic sentence?
- ☐ ☐ (3) Does the concluding paragraph restate the topic and review the ideas?
- ☐ ☐ (4) Does the essay stick to the topic?

Support
- ☐ ☐ (5) Do the paragraphs include specific details and examples that support the topic sentences?
- ☐ ☐ (6) Does the essay support the thesis statement?

Clarity
- ☐ ☐ (7) Is the main idea understandable?
- ☐ ☐ (8) Are the supporting ideas expressed clearly?

You can revise your essay during any of the POWER steps. For example, correct a misspelled word whenever you notice it.

Your answers to the questions tell you which parts of your essay need revising. For example, if your answer to question 1 is no, decide how to add a thesis statement or the essay topic. Use revision marks to add sentences. If your answer to question 4 is no, decide which sentences or phrases discuss things not directly related to the topic. Then cross them out.

Look at how one writer revised her essay on the topic assignment "State whether you think it is better to stay in one place or to move often and live in different places."

Main idea: *Living in one place has advantages and disadvantages.*

Many people live in one place their entire lives and enjoy it, but I prefer experiencing different places. Living in one place provides security, but there are many disadvantages to this lifestyle. Living in new places is exciting and educationel.

Living in one place for a long time does have some advantages. You know where everything is and have the security of a routine. If you need help, you can ask a friend or neighbor. ₍It is easy to cash checks and conduct other business because everyone knows you.

For me these advantages are overshadowed by the disadvantages of staying in one place. Especially in a small town, you can't escape your Educational and job opportunities are often limited. *past. Everyone knows everything about you. ₍The biggest disadvantage is that everything stays the same—to me that means boredom!*

Moving to a different city or town is an adventure. Everything will be unfamiliar to you. You will have new experiences you will have different things to see and do. Maybe you will be near mountains or on the ocean. You could learn to ski or surf. ~~But remember, long distance phone calls are expensive.~~ Moving can give you opportunities you didn't have before. Best of all, you will be able to meet a variety of people and make many new friends.

So brave! Find a place you think you'd like, then pack up and move. ~~Decide if you will move yourself or if you will hire a moving company.~~ You'll have many more exciting experiences than people who stay in one place all their lives.

When the writer began evaluating her essay, she noted her thesis statement, "Many people live in one place their entire lives and enjoy it, but I prefer experiencing different places." As she evaluated, she looked for ideas that did not relate to the topic. She found a sentence in the fourth paragraph and one in the last paragraph that did not seem to fit, so she crossed them out.

The writer also realized she had not included her idea about the advantage of getting checks cashed. So she added a sentence to the second paragraph about checks. In addition, she felt she had not given enough support to the disadvantages of living in one place, so she added a sentence about opportunities to her third paragraph.

When you revise your essay, compare it with your planning list of ideas. That will help you determine if you included all your ideas.

Read the following essay about the advantages and disadvantages of owning an automobile. Evaluate and revise the essay for its presentation of ideas. Use a copy of the Evaluation Check List on page 120 if you need to. Make your revisions right on the essay.

Millions of people own automobiles. Sometimes they like owning their cars. Other times they don't. As every car owner knows, there are distinct advantages and disadvantages to owning an automobile. I own a car and so does my brother.

Owning a car offers several very important advantages. A car provides easy transportation right from your home. You don't have to worry about bus routes or waiting for buses. Also, you can carry more things than you can carry on a bus.

Still another advantage to having a car is that it's fun. You can have a sound system in your car to listen to music. My favorite is country music. Driving along with the windows open and good music playing makes you feel alive.

While owning a car has advantages, it also has disadvantages. You have to get a driver's license. There is a test for this, and it can be difficult to pass. You also need car insurance, which costs money. The upkeep and gas for your car cost money, too. Sometimes you have to leave your car for repairs. This costs time and money.

Even though owning a car can cost you time and money, the advantages of owning a car outweigh these disadvantages. Bus riding is okay. My brother and I rode the bus everywhere before we got our cars. For convenience, fun, and carrying capacity, an automobile is a must.

Revising Your Use of the Conventions of English

After you make revisions to the ideas and organization of your essay, you can evaluate and revise your use of the conventions of English. To evaluate (POWER Step 4), you asked yourself this group of questions:

Yes	No	**Conventions of English**
☐	☐	(9) Are the ideas written in complete sentences?
☐	☐	(10) Is the grammar correct?
☐	☐	(11) Are punctuation marks used correctly?
☐	☐	(12) Are words spelled correctly?
☐	☐	(13) Are capital letters used correctly?

Your answers to the questions tell you which parts of your essay need correcting. For example, if you've written an incomplete sentence, correct the sentence fragment by adding a noun or a verb and drawing a caret to show where it should be inserted. If you've forgotten to use a comma between items in a list, put one in. If you've misspelled a word, cross it out and write it correctly above the misspelling.

Look again at the essay about living in one place versus moving to different places. The writer has finished the second revision step and has corrected her errors in the conventions of English. Her revision marks are in color.

Main idea: *Living in one place has advantages and disadvantages.*

Many people live in one place their entire lives and enjoy it, but I prefer experiencing different places. Living in one place provides security, but there are many disadvantages to this lifestyle. Living in new places is exciting and educational.

Living in one place for a long time does have some advantages. You know where everything is and have the security of a routine. If you need help, you can ask a friend or neighbor. It is easy to cash checks and conduct other business because everyone knows you.

For me these advantages are overshadowed by the disadvantages of staying in one place. Especially in a small town, you can't escape your past. Educational and job opportunities are often limited. Everyone knows everything about you. ^ The biggest disadvantage is that everything stays the same—to me that means boredom!

Moving to a different city or town is an adventure. Everything will be unfamiliar to you. You will have new experiences. You will have different things to see and do. Maybe you will be near mountains or on the ocean. You could learn to ski or surf. ~~But remember, long distance phone calls are expensive.~~ Moving can give you opportunities you didn't have before. Best of all, you will be able to meet a variety of people and make many new friends.

So ^be^ brave! Find a place you think you'd like, then pack up and move. ~~Decide if you will move yourself or if you will hire a moving company.~~ You'll have many more exciting experiences than people who stay in one place all their lives.

The writer noticed that she had misspelled the word <u>educational</u> in the first paragraph, so she crossed out the misspelling and <u>rewrote the word</u> correctly (see page 77). She found a run-on sentence in the fourth paragraph, so she added a period and capitalized the next word to make two sentences. Finally, she realized she had a sentence fragment at the beginning of the concluding paragraph, so she inserted a verb with a caret.

Her essay was now finished. By following the five POWER steps, she was able to write an effective five-paragraph essay.

Be sure to use all the POWER steps when you write the GED essay. You may allow more or less time for a step than the time suggested, but following the steps will help you write a better essay.

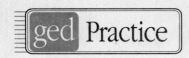

The following essay was written about the popularity of fast-food restaurants. Evaluate and revise the essay for its use of the conventions of English. Use a copy of the Evaluation Check List on page 120 if you need to. Make your revisions directly on the essay.

Over the past few years, there has been an increase in the number of fast-food restaurants across the country. Its easy to see why. The increase is due to their convenience, their prices, and the rising number of families where both husband and wife work outside the home.

Fast-food restaurants are conveniently located. They're built near homes by companies and along highways. In addition, they usually offer short menus you can make a quick, easy decision about what you want to order.

These restaurants also offer low prices. Hamburgers under a dollar. Salad bars are usually inexpensive, too. Also, if you eat at a fast-food restaurant, you don't spend money on food at home or on the gas or electricity to cook it.

Finaly, more and more families are made up of working couples. The husband and wife are tired when they come home and don't want to cook they want to spend time with their kids. Therfore, they get everybody into the car and head out to the nearest fast-food restaurant.

The poplarity of fast food and the increase in restaurants serving it are easy to understand. These restaurants offer tired, hungry people just what they want.

Revising an Essay

The following essay was written about winning money in a lottery. Evaluate and revise the essay for both its presentation of ideas and its use of the conventions of English. Use a copy of the Evaluation Check List on page 120 if you need to. Make your revisions directly on the essay.

I usually enter every contest or sweepstake that come along, so I have given much thought to what I would do if I really won something big. I have decided that if I won the State lottery, I would help my family and the needy first, and then I would have some fun.

My family could use some financial help. I would love to pay off my parent's home so that they would never have another house payment to make. Financing a house is extremely expensive these days. I would put money aside for my sister's children to go to colege. In addition, I would buy my brother and his wife a car so that they wouldn't have to ride the bus to work.

I would also give money to needy causes that I think are important. For example, cancer and AIDS research.

With the rest of the money, I would have a great time. I would travel to places I have never been. Every time I go to the bookstore I see all these books about travel. I would never cook another meal I would eat out every day in a diffrent restaurant. I would hire a maid so that I would never have to clean the house again. Finally, I would buy tickets to every concert every sports event and every new movie that comes to town.

Winning the lottery would be great for me and everyone else. Therefore, I will keep buying those lottery tickets

Here is the topic assignment you wrote an essay for on pages 52–53 and evaluated on page 71.

> Over the past few years, many people who were living in the country have moved to the city. At the same time, many people in the city have moved to the country.
>
> In a composition of about 200 words, state whether you think life is better in the country or in the city. Give specific examples to support your view.

First, revise the presentation of ideas in your essay. Use your answers to the first three groups of questions on the check list on page 71 to guide your revision.

Second, revise your use of the conventions of English. Use your answers to the last group of questions on the check list to help you find mistakes.

 Unit 6 MORE ON PREWRITING

P **Planning** Your Essay

O **Organizing** Your Essay

- ◆ **Brainstorming**
- ◆ **Asking Questions**
- ◆ **Using an Idea Circle**

W Writing Your Essay

- ◆ **Mapping**
- ◆ **Outlining**

E Evaluating Your Essay

R Revising Your Essay

By working through the five POWER steps in this program, you have learned a process for writing an essay for the GED test. In this unit, you will revisit POWER Steps 1 and 2 to learn more techniques for planning and organizing an essay. Because these steps come before the actual writing of the essay, they are called **prewriting steps.**

More Ways to Gather Ideas

Listing ideas and making an idea map are two good ways to gather ideas for an essay. But with some topic assignments, you may have a harder time thinking of ideas. When that happens, you might want to try a different technique to loosen up some ideas. Three more techniques to use to get your ideas flowing are brainstorming, asking questions, and using an idea circle.

Brainstorming

Brainstorming is similar to listing ideas. However, when you brainstorm, you think and write very quickly. Set a time limit for yourself and then write down all the ideas that come to mind about the topic. Don't take time to judge whether your ideas are good. And don't worry about spelling or capitalization. Just think about your topic and jot down everything that comes into your head. Think of brainstorming as a storm whirling in your brain and blowing your ideas out onto your paper.

After the time is up, stop brainstorming. Now is the time to be critical of your list. Look at the ideas you have written and evaluate them. Cross out ideas that seem out of place or that stray too far from the topic.

tip

Take no more than five minutes to brainstorm when you write a GED essay. You need additional time to go through the list, find the best ideas, and cross out the others.

Here is an example of what one student came up with using brainstorming. Read his list for the topic assignment "Why do so many people have pets?"

for company
all different kinds of pets
most people have dogs or
  cats
something to take care of
love and be loved
lot of lonely people in
  world
want something to do

pet shows
win prizes
stylish thing to do
want to impress people
something to own
pet's a possession
can have control over
can train to obey you
easier than training
  kids

good for kids
teaches them
  responsibility
teaches them about birth
  and death
can hunt with
beagles are good birders

The ideas are about pets, but many of the ideas don't focus on reasons for having a pet. The writer would need to cross out ideas that are off topic after evaluating them. You are more likely to get off-topic ideas when you brainstorm than when you carefully think out your list. When you brainstorm, allow more time to decide which ideas are worth keeping.

Another way to get ideas is to ask yourself questions about the topic—who, what, when, where, why, and how. You used this questioning technique in POWER Step 2 when you expanded your idea groups. It is also a good technique to use when you are stuck and can't think of any ideas.

Look at these ideas for the topic assignment "How does the weather affect people?"

Who? Everyone's affected. Young and old. Men and women. Me personally.

What? Outdoor plans can be affected. Travel. Sports like baseball. Vacations.

Where? Every place has both good and bad weather. Some places have good weather most of the time.

When? Wintertime especially bad. Spring and summer thunderstorms too. Rush hour affected by bad weather.

Why? Because weather's everywhere.

How? Moods—People feel blue when it's rainy, good when it's warm and sunny. Bad weather affects travel and outdoor activities. Kids can't play outside. Heating and cooling bills.

Not all the questions will relate to your topic. For example, answering where might not make sense if you are writing about the effects of watching TV because TV is almost everywhere; answering when might not make much sense if you are writing about climates in different parts of the country. However, by concentrating on one or two questions, you will usually get some ideas rolling.

Still another way to get ideas is to use an idea circle.

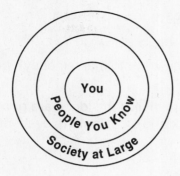

An **idea circle** is a diagram of nested circles that shows how widening groups of people are affected by something. In the center ring, tell how a topic relates to you personally. Then in the next ring, think about how it relates to the people around you—your family, relatives, friends, and coworkers—and write those ideas next. Finally, in the outer circle, think about how the topic relates to society at large and include those ideas.

Read the ideas a student wrote using an idea circle for the topic assignment, "What would life be like without television?"

For me: I probably watch too much anyway. Free me up to do other things. Work out. Spend time with my kids and wife. Talk to them, not just sit in front of the tube. Have real dinner conversation. Might try to go to a few baseball or football games.

For the people I know: Wife loves to watch news. Maybe she'd read newspaper? Kids watch too much now. They'd have to play games. Use their imagination.

For society: People wouldn't sit at home so much. Maybe go out to movies, restaurants. Probably better for the economy. Might even be friendlier to each other. Wouldn't feel so separate. If people are active, better for their health.

Practice gathering ideas using the three new techniques in this unit—brainstorming, questioning, and using an idea circle.

1. **Brainstorming topic assignment:** What are some ways to make money?

   a. Give yourself five minutes to brainstorm for ideas.
   b. List all the ideas that come to mind. Don't stop to think if the ideas are good or well written.
   c. At the end of five minutes, stop writing. Go back and cross out irrelevant or off-topic ideas.

   _____

   _____

   _____

   _____

   _____

   _____

   _____

   _____

   _____

2. **Questioning topic assignment:** What are some ways to spend money?

   Who? _____

   _____

   What? _____

   _____

   When? _____

   _____

   Where? _____

   _____

   Why? _____

   _____

   How? _____

   _____

3. **Idea circle topic assignment:** How important is it for people to be satisfied with their jobs?

How important is it for you to be satisfied with a job?

_____

_____

_____

_____

How important is it for the people you know to be satisfied with their jobs?

_____

_____

_____

_____

_____

How important is it to society at large for people to be satisfied with their jobs?

_____

_____

_____

_____

_____

More Ways to Organize

In POWER Step 2, you learned to organize your ideas by grouping them and finding a name or label for the group to show what the ideas have in common. You may find that there are other ways to organize ideas that are more helpful for you. For example, some people find it more helpful to map their ideas. Others prefer to outline.

Mapping

If you gather ideas by drawing an idea map, your ideas will already be organized. However, if you list ideas or use one of the planning techniques in this unit, you can organize the ideas by mapping them.

Mapping is a visual way to show the relationships between ideas. To map, write your main idea in the middle of your paper and circle it. Next, write the name for an idea group, circle it, and connect it to the main idea. Then list ideas that belong with that group on lines extending from the circle. Connect minor details and examples to the relevant supporting ideas. Continue with the next group until you map all your ideas.

When you finish mapping, you will have a diagram like this map showing the reasons people have pets. Find the main idea in the middle and the supporting groups that surround it.

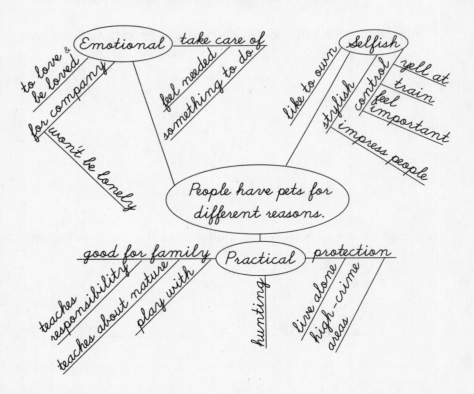

Mapping helps show how your groups of ideas relate to the main idea. But a map does not show the order that the ideas will follow in your essay. After you map, number the groups to show the order you select.

Outlining is another method of organizing. An outline is an ordered list of ideas that shows how ideas are related to each other. In an outline, numbers and letters identify ideas and show how they are classified.

To outline, use Roman numerals (I, II, III) to list the idea groups. Then below each Roman numeral group, use capital letters to list supporting ideas. Below each supporting idea, use Arabic numerals (1, 2, 3, and so on) to list minor details and examples.

Here is an outline of the same ideas mapped on page 88. Notice how the outline shows not only the relationships of ideas but also their order.

I. To Fill an Emotional Need
   A. For company so they won't be lonely
   B. To love and be loved
   C. Something to take care of
      1. Gives you something to do
      2. Makes you feel needed

II. For Practical Reasons
   A. Good for family to have pet
      1. Helps kids learn responsibility
      2. To play with
      3. Teaches about nature, birth, and death
   B. For protection
      1. People who live alone
      2. People who live in high-crime areas
   C. To hunt with

III. For Selfish Reasons
   A. Some people just like to own things
   B. Stylish thing to do—want to impress people
   C. Something to have control over
      1. Can yell at
      2. Can train to obey on command
      3. Makes you feel important

1. Map your ideas about ways to make money. Use the ideas you brainstormed on page 86. Use a copy of the blank idea map on page 119 if you prefer.

   a.   Write the main idea in the middle of the space and circle it.
   b.   Decide how you will group and name your ideas.
   c.   Write your first group name, circle it, and connect it to the main idea.
   d.   Write the details on lines extending from the circled group name.
   e.   Continue with the other ideas until you map them all.

2. Outline your ideas about job satisfaction. Use your ideas from the idea circle on page 87.

   a.   Write your main idea at the top of the space.
   b.   Decide how you will group and name your ideas.
   c.   Write Roman numeral I with your first group name.
   d.   Below Roman numeral I, use capital letters to write the supporting ideas for the group.
   e.   Below the capital letters, use Arabic numerals to identify details and examples.
   f.   Continue with the other ideas until you outline them all.

   _____

   _____

   _____

   _____

   _____

   _____

   _____

Write an essay using the five POWER steps.

TOPIC

Many people consider athletes to be heroes. Others think of movie stars or TV stars as heroes. Yet some people believe athletes and actors are celebrities and not true heroes.

What are the qualities of a true hero? In a composition of about 200 words, state your view. Be specific, and give examples.

POWER Step 1: **Plan** your essay. First, write your main idea. Then, to gather ideas, choose one of these techniques: brainstorming, asking questions, or using an idea circle.

POWER Step 2: **Organize** your ideas. Choose either mapping or outlining to help you organize.

POWER Step 3: **Write** your essay. Remember to keep your ideas in order and to write good introductory and concluding paragraphs.

POWER Steps 4 and 5: **Evaluate** and **revise** your essay. First, evaluate your presentation of ideas and rewrite any that need revising. Then proofread your essay for the conventions of English and correct any errors.

RAISING YOUR SCORE

P | Planning Your Essay

O | Organizing Your Essay

W | ## Writing Your Essay

- ◆ Using Transitions
- ◆ Including Facts and Opinions
- ◆ Using Precise Words

E | Evaluating Your Essay

R | Revising Your Essay

In POWER Steps 4 and 5, you learned to check for organization, support, and clarity in evaluating and revising an essay. In this unit, you will learn more techniques to strengthen an essay's organization, support, and clarity. By using these methods, you can increase your chances of getting a high score on the writing section of the GED.

Using Transitions

In learning ways to organize a GED essay, you saw how a word or phrase can signal order of importance or compare-contrast. These words or phrases are called transitions. **Transitions** help connect one idea to the next. They can emphasize your organization and help make your ideas clear. When you use transitions, your ideas flow from one sentence to the next or from one paragraph to the next. A reader can understand how the ideas relate to one another.

To see how transitions work, reread these paragraphs from the essay on seat belt laws that are ordered using **order of importance.** The transitions in color point out the order used and help show how the ideas are related.

> Seat belt laws are a source of money for cities. People ticketed for not wearing seat belts must pay fines, and this money can be used to improve traffic safety.
>
> Even more important, seat belt laws themselves improve traffic safety. Just by buckling up, people are reminded to drive more safely.
>
> But the most important reason that seat belt laws are wise is that they save lives. Countless numbers of people are alive today because they were wearing their seat belts when they had an accident. Countless more have been saved from serious injury.

Other transitions that show **order of importance** are better, best; to begin with, next in importance, mainly, finally; and first, second, next, last.

Reread these paragraphs using **contrast** from the essay on watching television. The transitions in color help connect the ideas and show how they are alike and different.

> There's no doubt that watching television can have positive effects. Adults can keep informed about current events by watching the evening news. They may even gain some practical knowledge about their health and other personal concerns. Children can learn from educational shows like Sesame Street. In addition, everyone can be entertained and even escape a little with the cartoons, comedies, movies, and action shows.
>
> On the other hand, watching television has some definite negative effects. Instead of just using it as a temporary escape, some people may watch television rather than deal with their problems. TV also keeps people from spending time with their family or from reading. In fact, it turns some people into couch potatoes keeping them from any physical activity.

Connect related ideas in a paragraph with a transition like *and, also, in addition, and even, too, another, similarly,* or *moreover*.

Connect ideas that are different by using a contrast transition like *on the other hand, instead of, however, but,* or *rather than*.

If you forget to use transitions when you write your essay, you can add them when you evaluate and revise.

In addition, television gives people a false sense of what life is like. They see commercials on TV and feel they must have what's being advertised. They see violence on shows and think modern life is more violent than it really is, or they may even think it's all right to act violently.

As you can see in the essays, you can use several kinds of transitions to tie ideas together. Transitions help you show a relationship, point out an example, tell a time sequence, explain a reason, or signal a contrast.

To Emphasize and Connect:	Use These Transitions:
1. ideas that are different (contrast)	◆ on one hand, although, instead, in spite of, in contrast, however, but, while, still, yet
2. ideas that are alike (compare)	◆ also, too, in addition, and
3. an example to a related idea	◆ for example, for instance, such as, like
4. a cause to an effect (cause-effect)	◆ because, so that, since, therefore, as a result
5. a point you want to make	◆ in fact, indeed, moreover

 Practice   Using Transitions

First, read this essay about leisure time effects without transitions. Then reread it and underline the best transitions to improve the connections between ideas and to show the order used in the essay.

Some people complain that they don't have enough leisure time. (Instead/For example), they should realize that more leisure time can have both good and bad effects upon their lives.

(On one hand/Therefore), more leisure time can improve the quality of many people's lives. They would have more time to spend with their families, to learn new things, to explore their creativity, and to travel. (On the other hand/As a result), family relationships would improve. (Instead/Additionally), people would become skilled in sports and hobbies.

(On the other hand/For example), too much leisure time can have some bad effects. People with little imagination or low self-esteem don't always do well with time on their hands. (In fact/So that), some people become depressed or bored. (However/Also), some join gangs or get into trouble with the law.

(In addition/In spite of), more leisure time can be expensive (because/although) all leisure activities—taking courses, traveling, sports—cost money. (In contrast/Moreover), it probably means fewer working hours. (And/After) that means less pay.

There are good and bad points to having more leisure time. (Last/However), if I had a choice, I'd take the extra time off!

Including Facts and Opinions

In POWER Step 3, you learned to use details and examples to support your topic sentences. Another good way to add support is to use facts and opinions.

A **fact** is a statement that can be proved true. You can check a fact with a reliable source, such as a reference book. A fact in a GED essay does not have to be a statistic or a specific name or detail; it can be a general statement about the topic that you know to be true.

An **opinion** is a statement of preference or belief. Although someone can agree or disagree with it, an opinion cannot be proved true. When a GED essay asks for your opinion, you write about your beliefs and feelings. You might include words of opinion that make value judgments such as beautiful, best, worthless, or important. Or you could include words that stress outcomes such as should, must, or ought.

Read this paragraph about the problem of illegal drugs. It contains three details supporting the main idea that drugs have become a serious problem.

> The drug problem has become serious. People are taking dangerous drugs, such as cocaine. They are also committing crimes to get money for drugs. In addition, some people are becoming drug dealers because of the money they can make.

Now read the paragraph with facts and opinions added to help support the main idea. The additional facts are in color, and the opinions are underlined in color.

> The drug problem has become serious. People are taking dangerous drugs, such as cocaine. They are also committing crimes to get money for drugs. Drug use and related crimes are rising every year. In addition, some people are becoming drug dealers because of the money they can make. This is an alarming and sad situation. Every year, more and more people lose their lives to drugs. Either they die of overdoses, or they die in violence connected to drugs. All these wasted lives are a tragedy.

It is not necessary to begin an opinion with "I believe" or "I think" or "In my opinion." Just state the opinion clearly and forcefully.

To think of facts to include in your essay, consider what you have heard and read about the topic—on the news; in newspapers, books, and magazines; or from other reliable sources. To think of opinions to include, consider how you personally feel, what you believe, and why you think as you do.

1. Suppose you are writing an essay on the need for taxes. Write <u>F</u> before the facts you could use to support ideas about taxes. Write <u>O</u> before the opinions.

_____ a. Polls show that many people want taxes to be changed.

_____ b. People who believe taxes are too high are mistaken.

_____ c. Taxes help provide aid for education and social programs.

_____ d. There is no more important use for tax dollars than schools.

_____ e. Tax dollars are used to build and maintain roads and bridges at the local, state, and national levels.

_____ f. Thousands of people use the national parks every year.

_____ g. The beauty of the national parks is worth the tax money spent on them.

2. Suppose you are writing an essay about ways to spend money on entertainment. For each supporting idea, write at least one fact and one opinion.

a. Movies   Fact: _____

_____

Opinion: _____

_____

b. Sports   Fact: _____

_____

Opinion: _____

_____

c. Hobbies   Fact: _____

_____

Opinion: _____

_____

Using Precise Words

Clarity is one of the features of writing you looked at to evaluate and revise your essay. **Clarity** refers to how clearly you present the ideas in your composition. Can a reader understand exactly what you mean? A good way to express ideas clearly is to use precise words rather than general terms. **Precise words** give the reader a mental picture of the ideas and a better understanding of what you mean. Precise language makes writing lively and interesting.

To understand how a few word changes can help clarity, read this paragraph about dressing for a job interview. Notice the words in color.

> When you go for a job interview, your appearance tells your potential employer something about you. If you look nice, you give the impression that you are serious about work. If you look bad, it suggests you don't care about work. So wear good clothes, and remember that your appearance tells something about you even before you talk.

When you read the paragraph, you may not be sure what the writer means about appearance. What exactly are good clothes? What does it mean to look nice?

Now read the paragraph with precise words replacing the more general terms. Notice how the precise words help you picture what the writer means.

> When you arrive for a job interview, your appearance tells your potential employer something about you. If you look neat and clean, you give the impression that you are serious about work. If you look sloppy or careless, it suggests you don't care about work. So wear clean, pressed, businesslike clothes, and remember that your appearance reveals something about you even before you utter a word.

To help you think of precise words to use:
- ◆ Picture in your mind what you want to discuss. Think of words that illustrate what you see.
- ◆ Ask yourself questions such as, How does this look? sound? smell? feel? taste? Use these sensory words in your descriptions.
- ◆ Visualize actions to help you find strong verbs like <u>claim</u>, <u>stroll</u>, and <u>crash</u> instead of <u>say</u>, <u>walk</u>, and <u>hit</u>.
- ◆ Think of words people use to describe similar ideas. Think of words you have heard on the news, on the radio, in movies, or in your class. Think of words you have read.

If you can't think of a precise word when you write, use a general term. Replace it with a precise word when you evaluate and revise.

Use all five senses— sight, sound, smell, taste, and touch— to help you think of precise words. And remember to use vivid verbs like *whispered* and *shouted* as well as vivid adjectives like *terrific* and *tragic*.

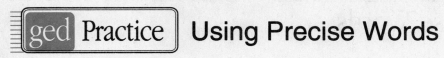

1. List precise words to describe each item. Answer the questions if you need help.

   a. city traffic (What does it look like? sound like? smell like? How does it feel to be in it? What actions take place in traffic? How would a TV reporter describe traffic?)

   _____   _____

   _____   _____

   _____   _____

   b. telephone (What does it sound like? How does using it make you feel? What actions take place while you use the telephone? How would a telephone be described in a book?)

   _____   _____

   _____   _____

   _____   _____

   c. money (What does it feel like to touch it? How does it look? How does having it make you feel? not having it? What can it do for you? How do other people describe money?)

   _____   _____

   _____   _____

   _____   _____

   d. summertime (How does it look? What are the smells, sounds, and tastes that go with it? What does it feel like? What actions take place in summertime? How is it described on the radio?)

   _____   _____

   _____   _____

   _____   _____

2. Write a more precise word (or words) to replace the underlined words.

   a. Listening to music is <u>nice</u>. _____

   b. Raising a child is <u>hard</u>. _____

   c. Crime is a <u>big</u> problem. _____

   d. Watching television can be <u>bad</u>. _____

Write an essay for the topic assignment below on your paper. Follow the five POWER steps:

Chapter	Steps	Time
Planning Your Essay (p. 14–23)	☐ Figure out the topic. ☐ Understand the instructions. ☐ Choose your main idea. ☐ Gather ideas.	5 minutes
Organizing Your Essay (p. 24–35)	☐ Group and name your ideas. ☐ Expand your groups. ☐ Order your groups.	5 minutes
Writing Your Essay (p. 36–53)	☐ Write your introduction. ☐ Write your body paragraphs. ☐ Write your conclusion.	25 minutes
Evaluating Your Essay (p. 54–71)	☐ Evaluate your ideas and organization. ☐ Evaluate your use of the conventions of English.	5 minutes
Revising Your Essay (p. 72–81)	☐ Revise your ideas and organization. ☐ Revise your use of the conventions of English.	5 minutes

As you write, try to use transitions, include facts and opinions, and write with precise language. Then as you evaluate and revise your essay, use more of these techniques to raise your score.

In the past, people wrote letters to communicate. Today many more people use the telephone.

Why do people prefer calling on the telephone to writing letters? What are the advantages of telephoning? Are there disadvantages? Tell your views in a composition of about 200 words. Be specific and give examples.

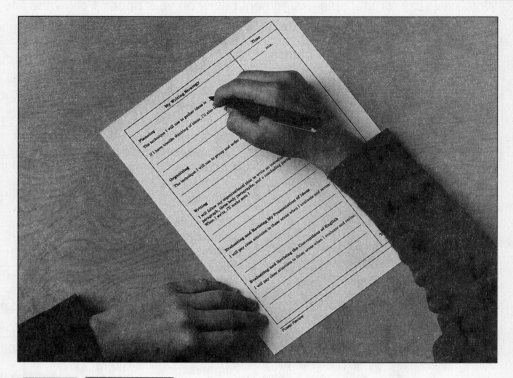

 Planning Your Essay

 Organizing Your Essay

 Writing Your Essay

 Evaluating Your Essay

 Revising Your Essay

In this unit, you will review the five-paragraph structure of an essay and the five POWER steps for writing one. You will practice writing and scoring GED essays, and you will plan your own strategy for writing your GED essay. By reviewing, practicing, and making a personal plan, you will increase your chances for a high score on the GED essay test.

The Five-Paragraph Essay

Remember that a strong response to a GED writing assignment takes five paragraphs. The five paragraphs make up three distinct parts of an essay. The three parts serve different purposes.

Introduction
One paragraph introduces the essay.

Thesis statement tells the main idea of the entire essay.
Preview sentences tell the approach to the topic.
Background sentences may be included to give information about the topic.

Body
Three paragraphs develop the topic by supporting the thesis statement.

Body Paragraph 1
Topic sentence tells the paragraph's main idea.
Supporting sentences give details, examples, facts, and opinions for the topic sentence.

Body Paragraph 2
Topic sentence tells the paragraph's main idea.
Supporting sentences give details, examples, facts, and opinions for the topic sentence.

Body Paragraph 3
Topic sentence tells the paragraph's main idea.
Supporting sentences give details, examples, facts, and opinions for the topic sentence.

Conclusion
One paragraph wraps up the essay.

Restates the thesis statement.
Reviews the main support.

The POWER Writing Process

Remember that writing an effective essay takes five main steps.

Step 1 Planning
Step 2 Organizing
Step 3 Writing
Step 4 Evaluating
Step 5 Revising

Each of the five steps involves smaller steps.

Step 1 **PLANNING** your essay involves:
- Figuring out the topic
- Understanding the instructions
- Choosing your main idea
- Gathering ideas

Step 2 **ORGANIZING** your essay involves:
- Grouping and naming your ideas
- Expanding your groups
- Ordering your groups

Step 3 **WRITING** your essay involves:
- Writing your introductory paragraph
- Writing your body paragraphs
- Writing your concluding paragraph

Step 4 **EVALUATING** your essay involves:
- Evaluating your ideas and organization
- Evaluating your use of the conventions of English

Step 5 **REVISING** your essay involves:
- Revising your ideas and organization
- Revising your use of the conventions of English

Write using the POWER steps as often as possible so the process is automatic. Then, when you take the GED essay test, you'll remember the five steps and will be able to follow them in order.

Prewriting and Writing

Remember that part of the planning step is understanding the instructions in the GED writing assignment. Key words in the instructions are clues to the kind of information you should include in your essay.

If the Instructions Say:	You Should Write About:
1. explain why	◆ causes or reasons
2. state a view present your opinion state your opinion	◆ what you think about an issue
3. identify describe	◆ qualities, traits, or characteristics
4. describe the effects of tell how might this affect	◆ good and bad effects
5. discuss the advantages and disadvantages	◆ the advantages (pros) and disadvantages (cons) of doing something

The information in a GED essay may usually be organized in one of two ways: (1) order of importance or (2) compare and/or contrast. The kind of information in the essay helps determine the best way to organize it.

If You Are Writing About:	Try This Organization:
1. causes or reasons	◆ order of importance
2. what you think about an issue	◆ order of importance
3. qualities of one thing	◆ order of importance
4. qualities of two things	◆ compare and contrast
5. good and bad effects	◆ contrast
6. advantages and disadvantages	◆ contrast

Here are some tips to follow when you write a GED essay:

- ◆ Stick to your plan. Use all the good ideas you come up with. Add any new ideas you think of.
- ◆ Write your essay with a ballpoint pen.
- ◆ Write neatly so your essay can be read. Don't worry about perfect handwriting because handwriting is not considered when scoring GED essays.
- ◆ Leave wide margins on your paper so you can add ideas when you revise.
- ◆ Leave space between the lines to correct errors.
- ◆ Keep an eye on the clock to allow enough time to finish.

Organization, Support, and Clarity

Remember that a good way to help improve the organization and clarity of an essay is to use transitions. Transitions show the connections between ideas. Transitions at the beginning of your paragraphs may indicate how the essay is organized.

If the Organization of Ideas Is:	Use These Transitions:
1. order of importance *(Discuss why you think...)*	◆ more important, most important, better, best, first, second, last
2. compare *(Explain how they are alike...)*	◆ like, also, similarly, in the same way
3. contrast *(Describe the good and bad effects...)*	◆ on one hand, on the other hand, in contrast, however, but, whereas, while, rather than, instead

At other times, you may want to connect ideas within a paragraph and show how they are related. Transitions can also help you make these connections.

To Emphasize and Connect:	Use These Transitions:
1. an example to a related idea	◆ for example, for instance, such as, like
2. ideas that are alike	◆ also, too, in addition, and
3. a cause to its related effect	◆ because, so that, since, therefore, as a result
4. a point you are making	◆ in fact, indeed, moreover
5. a sequence of events	◆ first, next, then, finally

To make sure your essay is clear to your reader, remember to include precise words. Here are some tips to help you use specific language:

- Use sensory words to describe how things feel, sound, smell, look, or taste.
- Picture the ideas in your head and describe exactly what you see.
- Ask yourself questions to help you come up with precise vocabulary.

Evaluating and Revising

Remember that to evaluate and revise the presentation of ideas in your essay, you consider three general areas—organization, support, and clarity. Read your essay carefully, but not too slowly, to evaluate these areas.

Yes No
Organization

☐ ☐ (1) Does the introductory paragraph include the essay topic and a thesis statement?

☐ ☐ (2) Does each body paragraph have a topic sentence and details related to the topic sentence?

☐ ☐ (3) Does the concluding paragraph restate the topic and review the ideas?

☐ ☐ (4) Does the essay stick to the topic?

Support

☐ ☐ (5) Do the paragraphs include specific details and examples that support the topic sentences?

☐ ☐ (6) Does the essay support the thesis statement?

Clarity

☐ ☐ (7) Is the main idea understandable?

☐ ☐ (8) Are the supporting ideas expressed clearly?

To evaluate how well you use language and follow the mechanics of writing, you look at another area of an essay—the conventions of English.

Conventions of English

☐ ☐ (9) Are the ideas written in complete sentences?

☐ ☐ (10) Is the grammar correct?

☐ ☐ (11) Are punctuation marks used correctly?

☐ ☐ (12) Are words spelled correctly?

☐ ☐ (13) Are capital letters used correctly?

When your essay needs improvement, use these revision methods:

◆ Cross out any unwanted words or phrases.

◆ Make corrections or add ideas between the lines or in the margin.

◆ Use a caret (^) to show where additions belong.

◆ Rewrite any part that is illegible or too messy to read.

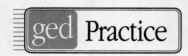

Because you cannot take an Evaluation Check List with you to the GED essay test, it's a good idea to remember as many of the criteria as you can when you evaluate.

What should you look for when you evaluate these areas? See if you can write a phrase or two to identify ideas about each element.

Organization

_____

_____

_____

_____

Support

_____

_____

_____

Clarity

_____

_____

Conventions of English

_____

_____

_____

_____

Now go back and compare your ideas with the check list on page 105. Make a note of those things you did not remember. As you continue to evaluate your writing, use the check list until you have a clear idea of the items to check.

Your Personal Writing Strategy

You have learned several techniques to help you follow the POWER writing process. Different techniques are presented here because every writer is different. To write your best GED essay, you need to determine the techniques that work best for you. You also need to decide which areas to work harder on. Then you can create your own writing strategy for scoring high on the GED essay test.

As you answer the questions below, think back to the essays and writing assignments you have completed. Use your experience to decide on the best strategy for you at each step in the process.

Gathering Ideas

Which of these techniques was the most useful for you in gathering ideas? Which seemed the second best way to gather ideas? Number the techniques below 1 and 2. Then write these choices in the chart on page 109.

_____ making a list

_____ drawing an idea map

_____ brainstorming

_____ asking questions

_____ using an idea circle

Organizing Ideas

Which of these techniques was the most helpful to you in grouping and ordering ideas? Check it off below. Write your best method for organizing ideas in the chart on page 109.

_____ circling and labeling in groups on the list

_____ rewriting the ideas in lists; naming the lists

_____ drawing an idea map

_____ outlining

Writing

Which of these tips do you have the most trouble remembering to follow? Which ones will help you write a good essay? Check them off and write them in the chart on page 109.

_____ write neatly and legibly with a ballpoint pen

_____ leave space between lines and in the margins for corrections

_____ add more ideas to the first ones I write down

_____ write quickly enough to finish on time

_____ stick to the organization plan

Which of these areas do you need to pay attention to when you evaluate and revise? Check any that you want to be sure to remember. Write them in the chart on page 109.

Presentation of Ideas

_____ including essay topic and background sentences in the introductory paragraph

_____ stating the thesis clearly in the introductory paragraph

_____ writing preview sentences in the introductory paragraph

_____ writing topic sentences for each body paragraph

_____ including details and examples, facts and opinions to support the topic sentence and the thesis statement

_____ sticking to the topic

_____ expressing ideas clearly with precise words and transitions

_____ restating the topic in the concluding paragraph

_____ reviewing the ideas in the concluding paragraph

Conventions of English

_____ using correct sentence structure

_____ correcting the grammar

_____ checking the punctuation

_____ looking over the spelling

_____ checking the capitalization

≡ Using Your Time

Each of the five POWER steps takes a certain amount of time. The chart on page 99 suggests an appropriate amount of time to spend on each step when you write your GED essay. However, the time frame that works best for you may be slightly different. Perhaps you take less time thinking of ideas but need more time to organize them. Or you may need more time to write your essay and less time to evaluate and revise it.

Write the times you think you need to spend on each step of the writing process. If you are not sure, use the times shown on page 99.

My Writing Strategy	Time

Planning

The technique I will use to gather ideas is _____

_____ .

If I have trouble thinking of ideas, I'll also try _____

_____ .

_____ min.

Organizing

The technique I will use to group and order my ideas is _____

_____

_____ .

_____ min.

Writing

I will follow my organizational plan to write an introductory paragraph, three body paragraphs, and a concluding paragraph.

When I write, I'll make sure I _____

_____ .

_____ min.

Evaluating and Revising My Presentation of Ideas

I will pay close attention to these areas when I evaluate and revise:

_____

_____

_____

_____ min.

Evaluating and Revising the Conventions of English

I will pay close attention to these areas when I evaluate and revise:

_____

_____

_____

_____ min.

Total 45   min.

Put your essay-test writing strategy to work. Follow the POWER writing steps and your writing strategy to write an essay for the topic assignment below. Use a copy of the Answer Sheet on pages 156–157 or your own paper. Time yourself on each step. Work for no more than 45 minutes.

People used to spend much of their leisure time reading books, newspapers, and magazines. These days, however, most people prefer watching television rather than reading.

Why do people prefer to watch television? Give your reasons in a composition of about 200 words. Be specific, and give examples.

After you have written your essay, check your writing strategy. Change any technique or problem area you feel you need to.

Check the times you listed on your strategy for each step. Decide if you could accomplish everything you needed to do in that amount of time. If not, go back and adjust the times on your writing strategy.

Scoring an Essay

Remember that GED scorers will read your essay once and then score it from 1 (lowest score) to 6 (highest score). (* is reserved for papers that are blank, unreadable, or off the topic.) The GED guidelines for scoring are found on page 55. In general, a paper falls into one category along this range of descriptions.

6   clear, appropriate organization; sophisticated ideas; effective support; vivid, precise writing; control of the conventions

5   clear organization; effective support; less fluent than a 6 paper; some errors in the conventions

4   evidence of organization; adequate support though not as extensive as a 5 or 6 paper; some errors in the conventions

3   some evidence of planning, but insufficient development; limited support; repeated weaknesses in the conventions

2   lack of organization; inadequate support; unfocused development; serious errors in the conventions

1   no purpose or development; no control of structure or the conventions; difficult or impossible to understand

*****   blank or illegible papers; essays written on a topic other than the one assigned

Here is an example of an essay with a score of 6. The essay was written for the topic assignment in the GED Practice on page 110.

Unlike people in the past, persons today who spend their leisure time reading are unusual. These days, people prefer watching television. Watching TV offers several advantages that reading books does not.

For one thing, watching TV is a social act. You can watch TV with your whole family, with a certain someone, or even with your pet dog. That feeling of togetherness is important these days, when busy lives sometimes keep people from spending time with each other. When you read, on the other hand, you're very much apart from others, even if they're in the same room with you.

A second reason people prefer watching TV is that they can do other things while they are watching. TV doesn't demand much attention, and your hands are totally free. You can sew on a button, cook a meal, or diaper a baby while keeping one eye on the TV screen. When you read, on the other hand, you might be able to free one hand to take a bite of dinner, but that's about all.

Finally, and perhaps the most important reason for people's preference, is that watching TV takes much less energy than reading a book. Although neither activity demands physical energy, reading requires mental energy. Your mind is at work. You have to concentrate on words in a book and imagine for yourself what people and places look like. Television shows do all that for you. You just have to keep your eyes open.

Therefore, it's not difficult to understand why people prefer watching television to reading books. Perhaps if their lives were less busy and tiring, they would enjoy spending the time and energy it takes to read.

 **Scoring Your Essay**

Read and score the essay you wrote for the GED Practice on page 110. Use the GED scoring range and the model essay beginning on page 111 as guides.

Follow the directions below, the POWER writing steps you have reviewed in this unit, and your writing strategy to write an essay on the assigned topic.

Directions

This part of the Writing Skills Test is intended to determine how well you write. You are asked to write an essay that explains something or presents an opinion on an issue. In preparing your essay, you should take the following steps:

1. Read carefully the directions and the essay topic given below.

2. Plan your essay carefully before you write.

3. Use scratch paper to make any notes.

4. Write your answer on separate paper.

5. Read carefully what you have written and make any changes that will improve your essay.

6. Check your paragraphs, sentence structure, spelling, punctuation, capitalization, and usage, and make any necessary corrections.

You will have 45 minutes to write on the topic below. Write legibly and use a ballpoint pen so that the evaluators will be able to read your writing.

"Nice guys finish last." Some people live their lives by that saying; others think it is wrong.

Do you agree or disagree with that saying? Write an essay of about 200 words presenting your view. Support it with specific examples from your experience or your observations of others.

Reprinted with permission of the American Council on Education.

Simulated Test A

WRITING SKILLS, PART II
Directions

Part II of the Writing Skills Test determines how well you write. You will have 45 minutes to write an essay that explains or presents an opinion or states a view on an issue. Follow these steps:

1. Carefully read the directions and the essay topic below.

2. Plan your essay before you write. Stick to the topic.

3. Use scratch paper to make notes.

4. Write your essay on a copy of the answer sheet on page 156. Write legibly and use a ballpoint pen so that your evaluator will be able to read your writing.

5. Read what you have written, and make any changes that will improve your essay.

6. Check your essay for sentence structure, spelling, punctuation, capitalization, and usage. Make any necessary corrections.

TOPIC A

Some apartment and condominium complex owners refuse to allow people with children under the age of eighteen and living at home to rent an apartment in their facilities. Some people have challenged in court the right of these "adult only" complexes to exclude renters because they have children.

Should apartment owners have the right to deny someone access to a rental unit because the potential renter has children? Write a composition of about 200 words in which you state your opinion. Provide reasons and examples to support your view.

Simulated Test B

Part II of the Writing Skills Test determines how well you write. You will have 45 minutes to write an essay that explains or presents an opinion or states a view on an issue. Follow these steps:

1. Carefully read the directions and the essay topic below.

2. Plan your essay before you write. Stick to the topic.

3. Use scratch paper to make notes.

4. Write your essay on a copy of the answer sheet on page 156. Write legibly and use a ballpoint pen so that your evaluator will be able to read your writing.

5. Read what you have written, and make any changes that will improve your essay.

6. Check your essay for sentence structure, spelling, punctuation, capitalization, and usage. Make any necessary corrections.

TOPIC B

Most states in the United States have passed laws raising the legal drinking age to twenty-one. Many people support this age limit, but others disagree. They think the age limit should be lowered. In their opinion, people should be able to drink, vote, and join the armed services at the same age.

In a composition of about 200 words, present your opinion. You may choose to agree or disagree with laws that make the legal drinking age twenty-one. Be sure to use specific examples to support your opinion.

Additional GED Topics

Use these topics to gain additional experience writing GED essays. Follow all the POWER Steps and take no more than 45 minutes to write your essays.

TOPIC 1

In the 1950s people began to hear about computers. Some people thought computers would never last. Others feared computers would take their jobs. Today computers are part of our lives.

Write a composition of about 200 words about how computers affect our lives. You may wish to deal with the good or bad effects, or both.

TOPIC 2

Few people ever say, "I have so much money that I just can't spend it all." More people are likely to pinch pennies. Getting by is easier if people learn wise ways of dealing with money.

Write a composition of about 200 words offering advice on stretching an income. You may want to include both "do's" and "don'ts."

TOPIC 3

Part of each TV hour is spent on ads. Newspapers and magazines are sometimes more than half ads. Ads seem to follow every song on the radio. It is not possible to avoid ads.

Write a composition of about 200 words stating the effects of ads on the buying public. You may consider the good effects or bad effects, or both.

TOPIC 4

Computer games, VCRs, large screen TVs, and cable TV have become common. More and more people have complete entertainment centers in their homes. These people have less and less need to leave the home for entertainment.

Write a composition of about 200 words stating what effects you think home entertainment has on modern life. You may talk about the good or bad effects, or both. Be specific. Use examples to support your view.

TOPIC 5

Each decade has its music. The 1950s brought Elvis and rock-and-roll. The 1960s were the Beatle years. Heavy metal and disco ruled the scene in the 1970s; punk rock, rockabilly, and rap emerged in the 1980s. In each decade, parents have feared that pop music would ruin their children.

Write a composition of about 200 words on the effects of pop music and culture on the young people of the late 1980s or the 1990s. You may deal with the good effects, the bad effects, or both.

TOPIC 6

In the 1960s cigarette packs began carrying a warning that smoking may be a health hazard. In the 1970s cigarette ads were banned from TV. Articles often appear in print about the dangers of smoking. Still people continue to smoke.

In a composition of 200 words tell why you think people continue doing things that are bad for them. You might choose a specific practice such as smoking, overeating, or not exercising.

TOPIC 7

Child abuse has become a big problem in our society. Not only is such abuse very harmful to the children involved, but these children are often scarred for life.

Write a composition of about 200 words telling what can be done to prevent child abuse.

TOPIC 8

Children are often asked, "What do you want to be when you grow up?" At age five, a child can easily choose. But career choices are harder for an adult because there are more choices to consider. After choosing a job field, an adult must choose a particular job—often making a choice between jobs that are very much alike.

Write a composition of about 200 words concerning what, besides the work one will be doing, one needs to consider when choosing a job.

TOPIC 9

In recent years some college athletes who hoped to be pros made headlines. When they were not drafted by a pro team, they found they were not prepared for any other job. They had counted on careers in sports. Some could not even read.

Write a composition of about 200 words concerning the need for education for athletes.

POWER Steps Check List

Writing an effective essay takes five main steps.

Step 1 Planning

Step 2 Organizing

Step 3 Writing

Step 4 Evaluating

Step 5 Revising

Each of the five steps involves smaller steps.

Step 1 PLANNING your essay

_____ Figure out the topic

_____ Understand the instructions

_____ Choose your main idea

_____ Gather ideas

Step 2 ORGANIZING your essay

_____ Group and name your ideas

_____ Expand your groups

_____ Order your groups

Step 3 WRITING your essay

_____ Write your introduction

_____ Write your body paragraphs

_____ Write your conclusion

Step 4 EVALUATING your essay

_____ Evaluate your ideas and organization

_____ Evaluate your use of the conventions of English

Step 5 REVISING your essay

_____ Revise your ideas and organization

_____ Revise your use of the conventions of English

© 1996 Steck-Vaughn Company. *GED The Essay.* Permission granted to reproduce for classroom use.

≡Idea Map Form

Evaluation Check List

Yes	No		
			Organization
☐	☐	(1)	Does the introductory paragraph include the essay topic and a thesis statement?
☐	☐	(2)	Does each body paragraph have a topic sentence and details related to the topic sentence?
☐	☐	(3)	Does the concluding paragraph restate the topic and review the ideas?
☐	☐	(4)	Does the essay stick to the topic?

Support

☐	☐	(5)	Do the paragraphs include specific details and examples that support the topic sentences?
☐	☐	(6)	Does the essay support the thesis statement?

Clarity

☐	☐	(7)	Is the main idea understandable?
☐	☐	(8)	Are the supporting ideas expressed clearly?

Conventions of English

☐	☐	(9)	Are the ideas written in complete sentences?
☐	☐	(10)	Is the grammar correct?
☐	☐	(11)	Are punctuation marks used correctly?
☐	☐	(12)	Are words spelled correctly?
☐	☐	(13)	Are capital letters used correctly?

Revision Methods

Cross out any unwanted words or phrases.
Make corrections or add ideas between the lines or in the margin.
Use a caret (^) to show where additions belong.
Rewrite any part that is illegible or too messy to read.

Writer's Handbook

Sentence Fragments

A **sentence** is a group of words that expresses a complete thought. A sentence must have a subject and a verb. The **subject** tells who or what does the action. The **verb** is a word that shows action or state of being. Read these sentences that show the subject and the verb marked with an <u>s</u> and a <u>v</u>.

Many people like ice cream.   Oak trees grow very tall.
      s   **v**   **s**   **v**

A **fragment** is a group of words that does not express a complete thought, but ends with a period. A fragment is usually an error.

A sentence fragment may be corrected in two ways. One way is to add the fragment to another complete sentence. The second way is to add words to the fragment to make it into a complete sentence. Notice that in the examples below the fragment, or error, has been underlined.

Fragment: Some people have unusual pets. <u>Like lizards and snakes.</u>

Correction: Some people have unusual pets. Lizards and snakes are two kinds of unusual pets.
(Add words to the fragment.)

Fragment: <u>After finishing the project.</u> The workers went home.

Correction: After finishing the project, the workers went home.
(Add the fragment to another sentence.)

Fragment: <u>Although I'm not hungry yet.</u> Our lunch break is at noon.

Correction: Although I'm not hungry yet, our lunch break is at noon.
(Add the fragment to another sentence.)

Fragment: Peter is an experienced hiker. <u>Hikes every weekend on trails near his house.</u>

Correction: Peter is an experienced hiker. He hikes every weekend on trails near his house.
(Add words to the fragment.)

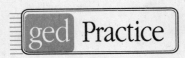

Sentence Fragments

Correct the sentence fragments by adding words to make complete sentences. There is more than one way to correct the fragments. Your answer is correct if your sentence contains a complete thought.

Fragment: Working hard for a living.

Correction: I am working hard for a living.

Correction: Working hard for a living, I get tired by evening.

1. Getting out of the habit of smoking.

   _____

   _____

2. Going to the movies this evening.

   _____

   _____

3. After the Super Bowl Game.

   _____

   _____

4. The Dallas Cowboys and the New York Giants.

   _____

   _____

5. After playing baseball for several years.

   _____

   _____

6. Like sports and hobbies.

   _____

   _____

Run-on Sentences

A **run-on sentence** is two sentences put together as if they were only one sentence. A run-on is an error in sentence structure. A run-on has two subjects and two verbs. It expresses two complete thoughts. There are two types of run-ons. One has two complete thoughts joined by a comma. The other has two complete thoughts joined with no punctuation at all.

Here are two ways to correct run-ons. One way is to put a period between the two parts. Another way is to use a comma and a **conjunction** (joining word) such as and, but, or, nor, so, for, or yet. Read the run-ons below. The verbs are underlined in color.

Run-on: Many children enjoy summer vacation, these same children may enjoy school, too.

Correction: Many children enjoy summer vacation. These same children may enjoy school, too.

Run-on: Many children enjoy summer vacation these same children may enjoy school, too.

Correction: Many children enjoy summer vacation, but these same children may enjoy school, too.

Run-on: Some people fear burglars, these people may have big guard dogs for protection.

Correction: Some people fear burglars. These people may have big guard dogs for protection.

Run-on: Some people fear burglars these people may have big guard dogs for protection.

Correction: Some people fear burglars, so these people may have big guard dogs for protection.

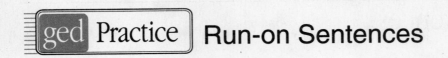

Correct the following run-on sentences in one of two ways — either separate the two thoughts by adding a period and a capital letter, or add a comma and a conjunction.

1. The team had lost the game the players were not happy.

   _____

   _____

2. Most children do not go to school all year they have vacation in the summer.

   _____

   _____

3. My mother likes movies she does not like television very much.

   _____

   _____

4. My friend lived in Georgia she liked the warm weather.

   _____

   _____

5. Some people have many pets others have no pets at all.

   _____

   _____

6. I worked hard at my job I did not get a raise.

   _____

   _____

Capitalization

1. Always capitalize the **first word** of a sentence.

   Tomorrow is Saturday.
   It is going to be a busy day.

2. Always capitalize the **pronoun I**.

   Juan and I are brothers.
   I am the oldest of three children.

3. Always capitalize the **names** of people, groups, nationalities, places, and events.

Dolly Parton	the Democrats	the Rolling Stones
French people	Canada	New England
Rocky Mountains	Elm Street	the Watermelon Festival

4. Always capitalize the **days** of the week, the **months** of the year, and **holidays**. Do not capitalize the seasons.

Tuesday	April	Christmas
Memorial Day	New Year's	winter

5. Always capitalize the **first word** and all **important words** in **titles** of songs, magazines, books, newspapers, movies, and television programs. Do not capitalize short prepositions or articles in a title.

"The Star-Spangled Banner"	Time magazine
The Adventures of Tom Sawyer	Chicago Tribune
Schindler's List	Murder, She Wrote

6. Always capitalize President when referring to the **President of a country**. Capitalize **other titles** only when they are used before a name, but not when they are used alone.

President Clinton	the President of the U.S.
Senator Wilson	the senator from Ohio
Dr. John Wilson	the doctor at the clinic

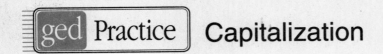

In the sentences below, circle the words that should be capitalized.

1. many kids today watch cartoons like <u>bugs bunny</u> on saturday mornings.

2. the american pioneers took many months to travel to the west in their covered wagons.

3. today i can drive my car from new york to san francisco in less than a week.

4. an article in the <u>new york times</u> reported that several doctors, including dr. howard bookman, think young children should use their imaginations instead of watching television.

5. school children have vacation in the winter months of november and december for the thanksgiving and christmas holidays.

6. do children still read <u>the adventures of huckleberry finn</u> and watch reruns of <u>the waltons</u>?

7. the humane society takes in stray animals.

8. if the boston city council lets the boston symphony orchestra play in the park, should michael jackson be allowed to perform there, too?

9. i have appointments to see my doctor, my lawyer, and my dentist, dr. james street.

10. i hope to travel to france someday to see the arch of triumph and the eiffel tower.

11. aunt kate, who visits every thanksgiving, is my mother's sister.

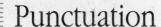# Punctuation

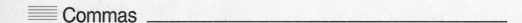Commas

Commas are like road signs. They show the reader when to pause to follow the meaning of a sentence.

1. Put a comma between **items in a series.**

   The recipe calls for potatoes, onions, and cheese.
   Steve likes playing ball, jogging with his dog, and swimming.

2. Put commas both between and after the parts of **dates** and **addresses**. Don't use a comma between the month and year when they are used alone.

   On November 22, 1963, President Kennedy was assassinated in Dallas, Texas.
   She moved to 1487 Key Largo Drive, Sarasota, Florida, in December 1994.

3. Put a comma between two complete **sentences joined by a conjunction** (like <u>and</u>, <u>but</u>, or <u>so</u>).

   The young children played on the beach, and the older ones swam in the lake.

Apostrophes

Another form of punctuation is the **apostrophe**.

1. Use an apostrophe to show **ownership**. Where you put the apostrophe depends upon whether you are talking about **one** or **more than one** person or thing.

   <u>Only One</u>   <u>More Than One</u>
   my doctor's house (one doctor)   doctors' houses (a few doctors)

2. Use an apostrophe to show letters have been omitted in a **contraction**.

   do not—don't   we have—we've   let us—let's

 Commas

Put commas where they belong in the following sentences.

1. Radio television and movies were all invented in the last 100 years.

2. The hills are steep and the valleys are deep.

3. Happiness may come from good health work you enjoy and a loving family.

4. I work for the city but my brother works for the state.

5. Her new address is 200 W. Maple Smithville Ohio.

6. Our last meeting was Tuesday September 8 1986 at 6:30 p.m.

7. He read the instructions too quickly so he forgot which step to do first.

8. The kitchen was equipped with pots pans dishes and utensils.

9. He enjoys baking bread but he doesn't have much time for it.

 Apostrophes

In each of the following sentences, circle the words with the apostrophe placed correctly.

1. I went to my (friend's/friends') house after work, but he (wa'snt/wasn't) there.

2. (Don't/Do'nt) expect your (car's/cars') engine to stay in good condition without regular maintenance.

3. (Theyr'e/They're) interested in whether the two (program's/programs') ratings improved.

4. My (lawyer's/lawyers') office is very large for just one person.

5. The (worker's/workers') tools were left on their benches during the fire drill.

6. (We've/W'eve) run out of paper for the copier again.

7. (W'ell/We'll) order more when I find the (store's/stores') telephone number.

8. (H'es/He's) going to paint his (mothers'/mother's) house for her.

9. (Wer'e/We're) looking for a good used car to replace the (family's/familys') old one.

10. (He's/H'es) coaching his youngest (son's/sons') soccer team.

Spelling

1. Words that **sound alike** but are **not spelled alike** are sometimes confused. Pay attention to what each word means. Remember the spelling and meaning of each word. Look at the sound-alike words below.

its	The cat licks <u>its</u> long fur.	(shows ownership)
it's	<u>It's</u> a simple idea.	(contraction for it is)
your	It is <u>your</u> choice.	(shows ownership)
you're	Tell me where <u>you're</u> going.	(contraction for you are)
their	<u>Their</u> plan was confusing.	(shows ownership)
there	The car is over <u>there</u>.	(tells where)
they're	<u>They're</u> riding with me.	(contraction for they are)
to	She went <u>to</u> the concert.	(tells where)
too	She wanted ice cream, <u>too</u>.	(also)
two	<u>Two</u> heads are better than one.	(a number)

2. Spelling errors often occur in words that contain the letter combinations **-ie** or **-ei**. Use -<u>i</u> before -<u>e</u>, except after the letter <u>c</u>- or when the letters sound as long <u>a</u>, as in <u>neighbor</u> or <u>weigh</u>.

ie	p<u>ie</u>	y<u>ie</u>ld	bel<u>ie</u>ve
ei after c	rec<u>ei</u>ve	dec<u>ei</u>t	c<u>ei</u>ling
ei sounds as a	n<u>ei</u>ghbor	w<u>ei</u>gh	fr<u>ei</u>ght

There are some **exceptions** to the above rules.

<u>ei</u>ther	h<u>ei</u>ght	sc<u>ie</u>nce	anc<u>ie</u>nt
n<u>ei</u>ther	l<u>ei</u>sure	consc<u>ie</u>nce	w<u>ei</u>rd
s<u>ei</u>ze	s<u>ei</u>zure	spec<u>ie</u>s	

 **Spelling: Sound-Alike Words**

In the sentences below, circle the sound-alike words that are spelled correctly according to the meaning in the sentence.

1. The nicest part of (their/they're/there) new house is (its/it's) big front porch.

2. The solution to (your/you're) problem depends upon what (their/they're/there) boss says.

3. Yesterday the committee made (its/it's) decision to allow members to bring (their/they're/there) husbands or wives, (to/too/two).

4. If (your/you're) relatives want to visit you during the holidays, you can take (to/too/two) weeks of vacation.

5. (Its/It's) easy to see from (your/you're) red eyes that (your/you're) tired today.

6. (Their/They're/There) complaining that (its/it's) (to/too/two) cold in (their/they're/there).

7. (Two/Too/To) other women wanted (two/too/to) go to the game, (two/too/to).

8. (Its/It's) not (two/too/to) late (two/too/to) sign up for the summer baseball teams.

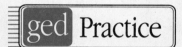 **Spelling: Words with -ie and -ei**

Complete the words in each sentence by adding -ei or -ie.

1. Michelle wanted to w____gh herself on the doctor's scale.

2. Ron has two n____ces and four nephews.

3. I rec____ved a letter from an old friend last week.

4. Is September the ____ghth month or the ninth?

5. What did he mean when he said s____ze the day?

6. I'm very rel____ved that I finished writing the essay in time.

7. Take a p____ce of paper with you to write notes on.

8. What a w____rd and unusual painting that is!

9. There's already a water stain on the new c____ling.

10. Ana's fr____nd gave her a pair of beautiful earrings for p____rced ears.

---

3. Spelling errors often occur when an **ending is added** to a word. If a word ends in a **consonant and an e** (such as ride or smile), **drop the e** before adding an ending that begins with a vowel.

ride + -ing = riding   smile + -ing = smiling
ride + -er = rider   smile + -ed = smiled

4. If a one-syllable word uses a **consonant-vowel-consonant** pattern (such as get or run), **double the final consonant** before adding an ending that begins with a vowel.

get + -ing = getting   run + -ing = running
wet + -er = wetter   run + -er = runner

5. Spelling errors often occur when an ending is added to a word ending in -y. If a word ends in a **consonant and -y** (such as baby or happy), **change the -y to -i** before adding the ending.

consonant and -y	happy	happiness
	worry	worried
	mystery	mysterious

But the ending **-ing** is an **exception** to the rule.

-ing exception	terrify	terrifying
	worry	worrying

6. If a word ends in a **vowel and -y** (such as joy or boy), **keep the -y** before adding the ending.

vowel and -y	joy	joyful
	boy	boyhood

7. If a word is a **one-syllable word**, **keep the** -y before adding the ending.

one-syllable	shy	shyness

The ending **-ed** is an **exception**.

-ed exception	try	tried

Spelling: Words with Suffixes

Write the correct spelling for each word with a suffix (ending) added.

1. drop + -ing _____
2. hope + -ing _____
3. date + -ing _____
4. stop + -ed _____
5. sit + -ing _____
6. give + -ing _____
7. rob + -ed _____
8. swim + -ing _____
9. hop + -ed _____
10. cut + -ing _____

Spelling: -y Words with Suffixes

Write the correct spelling for each word with a suffix (ending) added.

1. easy + -ly _____
2. try + -ed _____
3. cry + -ing _____
4. supply + -ing _____
5. rely + -able _____
6. lazy + -ness _____
7. satisfy + -ed _____
8. busy + -er _____
9. fifty + -eth _____
10. delay + -ed _____

Sample Essays

Essay 1

The modern day automobile has several affects , ~~on our civilization~~, both positive and negative, on our civilization. On a positive viewpoint, the automobile can be considered essential to our lifestyle. Today's world is much more fast-moving than before. People have deadlines to meet, and, without the use of the automobile, it would be difficult to uphold these obligations. Also, the transportation of goods makes the automobile neccessary. For example, if a company were to ship its goods over a ~~fif~~ fifteen mile distance, it would be much more economical to use ~~or a~~ truck rather than a train or plane. The automobile also gives its owner a sence of freedom. If an owner of an automobile has a weekend off, for. instance, he can ~~take~~ that short ~~trip for the~~ vacation he would not have had if he did not have an automobile. In these ways, the automobile tends to ~~be~~ serve ~~its~~ civilization well. ~~It~~ does, however, have its drawbacks.

The automobile has caused ~~&~~ several problems in today's society. It has ~~caused~~ unquestionably added to the problem of ~~&~~ pollution. The exhaust of an automobile has increased the problem of air pollution considerably. The installation of catylitic converters and the installation of emission controls has lessened the problem, but has by no means solved it. Noise pollution is another situation to be ~~&~~ recognized. A crowded free-way during rush hour can be very disturbing to any nearby residents. I have seen no solution to this problem, for, while ~~you~~ it is possible to make an engine quieter, it is impossible to keep a motorist from blowing his horn. Traffic fatalities must also be considered. ~~By letting~~ Lowering the national speed-limit to 55 miles per hour has helped, but again, this has not solved the problem. By reviewing these arguments, the automobile may be considered a hazzard to modern day civilization.

All in all, while the automobile has aided our modern world in many ways, it still has its drawbacks. If these drawbacks can be ironed out, the automobile may be considered a tremendous asset by any standards.

_JH_

Automobile has been a positive effects in many peoples life today. It is a deep pleasure to a lot of us. Most of all about automobile is a good use for elders people who can't get around. It is also a good use for traveling because it is very hard to walk to Calforina, but when there is an automobile around. you have it made. I think an automobile is one of the best thing a human can have. In case of an emeregency, there are ambulance, police cars, and etc. It also can get you to the ~~body~~ hosipital most easy, and may get you there in time enough to save your life. There are many kinds of automobiles in the world's today. I think they are very important in some ways, like grocery shopping, going to work, and etc. Automobile is also a negative effect in many people life today, most of all it deals with teenage, there are more teenage involved in automobile accident in the world today, because of Alchol beverages. A automobile is nothing to play around with. It is a dangerous vechile which have destoryed many people life you this world today. When you are drinking alchol don't drive an automobile because it is leading you on to death. It is a sudden way you are suspose to handled a vechile, such as the way you speed. Most of the automobile comes from racing too, like I said an automobile is nothing to play around with. For parents they should have safety in the case such when they have a little baby with them, they should have a car seat for the baby, It is against the law to have a baby while driving. That cause an automobile accident. Some Automobile are missed used by many peoples, because they don't know about automobile and the way they can harm you. You have to be very carefully when you are about to get your very on vechile, be very sure to have all parts of the vechile checked by a meachine, because anything could be wrong with the automobile. so you have to be very careful with them, because they will ~~bad~~ you on to death.

Essay 3

The automobile is a product of human ingenuity. It was made, ~~xxx~~ like every thing else, to preoccupy us, to distract us from reality. The man who made it is rich and happy. The man who crashed it didn't care. We must understand that all things put on this disgusting, ~~xxxx~~ Evil world was created to keep us busy or playing so that we don't have time to think about who made us and why he did it. We know that we are here and that's all we need to know As long as we have toys to play with. We know that us being the highest form of life, every thing IN OUR power including inferior people, Animals, And machines were maidE FoR personal gain and superiority. Everything we own and Everybody we know will either be used or will take advantage of someone not as great. Who EVER made us is more powerful than we are or he couldn't have created us therefore we too ARE being used. Just By living we are satisfying someone else's needs. We were meant to be born to live an average life then to die satisfied and content. If we do that we are serving the purpose of our Dictator Creator. We will have succeded in carrying out his plan. He will have succeded in using us. He continues to mislead us. We don't why we were made and where we will go after we die because he doesn't want us to know. People think they have life great and should be satisfied with what they have it. But people starving in other countries don't know how bad they have it because they don't know of our lives. God made people less fortunate because the people who have it better will think they really have it great and they think who ever made them is Just as great. But we don't have someone to really compare ourselves to we won't live long enough to see what great really is If we go by our creators plan. We must defy his plan and refuse to conform will his plan. We must not be satisfied with

We must not carry out his orders.
We must do the one thing that
he doesn't want us to. IF the
things I bought didn't serve there purpose
they would be useless. IF I didn't
serve my creator purpose I would
the n be useless too him and he would
be deprived of a servant. We must
turn the swords upon ourselves and
decide our own FAte INstead
living a story made to ENtertain
an Evil Nothing.

The Devil is never a MAker

But the Less that you give
MAkes you A tAker.
But it goes ON and ON and
ON.
Think about It hArd

Answers and Explanations

UNIT 1: PLANNING

GED Practice: Figuring Out the Topic (page 16)

For each item, draw a box around the first paragraph in the writing assignment as background information.

1. **Topic:** whether or not you think employers should supply child care for their employees.

   Instructions: Write a composition of about 200 words; be specific and use examples to support your view.

2. **Topic:** the effects of mandatory drug testing on employees.

   Instructions: In a composition of about 200 words describe the effects. You may wish to describe the positive effects, the negative effects, or both. Use specific examples to support your opinion.

3. **Topic:** How important is having a GED or a high-school diploma when you apply for a job?

   Instructions: In an essay of about 200 words, tell your opinion. Use specific examples to support your view.

4. **Topic:** how you think cigarette advertising should be handled. Should all ads for cigarettes be banned?

   Instructions: In an essay of about 200 words, support your opinion with specific examples.

GED Practice: Understanding the Instructions (pages 17–18)

1. **Instructions:** In a composition of 200 words, state the reasons; support your opinion with specific examples.

   Kind of information: tell what you think about an issue

2. **Instructions:** Write a composition of 200 words that describes both the negative and positive effects. Be specific and use examples.

   Kind of information: write about causes and effects

3. **Instructions:** In a composition of about 200 words, state your opinion. Use specific examples to support your point of view.

   Kind of information: tell what you think about an issue

4. **Instructions:** Write a composition of about 200 words describing the good points, the bad points, or both. Be specific, and use examples to support your views.

   Kind of information: give reasons or explain facts about an issue

5. **Instructions:** In a composition of 200 words, describe the effects. You may describe the good or bad effects, or both. Be specific, and use examples to support your views.

   Kind of information: write about causes and effects

GED Practice: Choosing Your Main Idea (page 19)

Many answers are possible. Here are some examples.

1. **Topic:** whether you think life is better in the country or in the city.

   Main idea: Living in the city has given me several benefits.

2. **Topic:** the effects of drug testing on employees.

   Main idea: Drug testing in the workplace causes good effects as well as bad effects.

3. **Topic:** How important is it to have a GED or a high-school diploma when you apply for a job?

   Main idea: One of the most important things in applying for a job is having a GED or a high-school diploma.

GED Practice: Listing Ideas (page 21)

Many answers are possible. Here are a few ideas.

1. **Ideas:** can communicate quickly; can communicate on the go; don't have to stay in one place to get messages; won't miss getting important messages on time; no excuses for not getting in touch with someone; doctors, emergency personnel, and other business people can respond to emergencies quickly

2. **Ideas:** lyrics are violent; songs promote unhealthy emotional and social attitudes; lyrics promote violence toward women; words promote drug use; lyrics promote violence toward police and authorities; music is repetitious and harsh

3. **Ideas:** everyone deserves to be healthy; health care costs have skyrocketed; unfair to some people for insurance costs to be so high; must work for a large company to have reasonable rates on health insurance; people who are sick can't get health insurance

4. **Ideas:** employers expect employees to be able to handle job tasks; can't compete with employees who are educated; jobs go to the best qualified; employers want their companies and their products to compete in world markets

GED Practice: Writing Idea Maps (page 22)

There are many possible answers. Show your idea maps to your teacher or another person.

GED Review: Unit 1: Planning (page 23)

A. **Background:** Over the past few years, many people who were living in the country have moved to the city. At the same time, many people in the city have moved to the country.

   Topic: whether you think life is better in the country or in the city.

   Instructions: In a composition of about 200 words, state what you think. Give specific examples to support your view.

B. **Kind of information:** tell what you think about an issue

C. Many answers are possible. Here is an example.

   Main idea: Life in the country is better than life in the city.

D. Many answers are possible. Here is an example.

   Ideas: life is simpler; people have closer ties to one another; houses cost less; people don't have to spend so much time in traffic; people know their neighbors; people can depend on each other; fewer problems in schools and with gangs; fewer problems with drugs; fewer problems with violence

UNIT 2: ORGANIZING
GED Practice: Grouping Ideas (page 27)

1.
	Pros
Practical Benefits	**Emotional/Social Benefits**
can learn things	have fun
can develop new skills	relieves stress
may discover a talent	may meet people with similar interests, make friends

Cons

may spend too much time away from family
may spend too much money
may neglect things that need to be done

Cross out <u>bowling is my hobby</u>.

GED Practice: Grouping Your Ideas (page 28)

Many answers are possible. Here are some ideas.

Ideas: pets keep people company; pets don't argue with their owners; pets require only occasional petting to keep them satisfied; pets don't eat much; pets don't require clothing, furniture, or personal items; pets don't have many expenses; dogs and cats snuggle up with their owners without asking much in return; pets miss their owners and greet them when they return; pets don't require their owners to communicate with them; pets are loyal

Groups of Ideas:
Group 1: pets aren't expensive to keep: pets don't eat much; pets don't require clothing, furniture, or personal items; pets don't have many expenses

Group 2: pets aren't fussy: pets require only occasional petting to keep them satisfied; dogs and cats snuggle up with their owners without asking much in return; pets miss their owners and greet them when they return

Group 3: pets are easy to communicate with: pets keep people company; pets don't argue with their owners; pets don't require their owners to communicate with them; pets are loyal

GED Practice: Expanding Groups (page 30)

Many answers are possible. Here are some examples.

1. **Benefits:** anyone can do it, including people with paralysis; good workout for the heart and lungs; relief from heat

   Little Equipment: goggles; swim fins

   Ease and Convenience: heated pools; lakes, ponds, rivers, and oceans

2. **Personal:** feeling of accomplishment; feel comfortable around educated people

   Job-related: feel good about applying for higher paying jobs; can expect more promotions

   Educational: can compete with other graduates; can read and understand more recreational reading materials

GED Practice: Expanding Your Groups (page 31)

Many answers are possible. Share your work with your teacher or another student.

GED Practice: Ordering Groups (page 34)

Many answers are possible. Here are some examples.

1. **1** Little Equipment, **2** Ease & Convenience, **3** Benefits

2. **Main Idea:** Passing the GED would give a person many advantages.
   1 Educational Reasons, **2** Job-related Reasons, **3** Personal Reasons

3. There is more than one correct response. Share your work with your teacher or another student.

GED Review: Unit 2: Organizing (page 35)

There is more than one way to group, expand, and order ideas. Share your work with your teacher or another student.

UNIT 3: WRITING
GED Practice: Paragraphs and Topic Sentences (page 41)

1. **a.** good work habits

   b. A good worker is someone who understands how important it is not to be absent too often and who gets the job done.

   c. people lose jobs because they don't show up for work or don't work hard enough; managers need workers they can count on to show up; employers don't tolerate workers who sit around visiting

2. **a.** the endangered bald eagle

   b. It is ironic that Americans are directly responsible for making the bald eagle, their national bird, an endangered species.

   c. people have developed land where eagles nest; they've polluted water, poisoning fish eaten by eagles; hunters and trappers killed eagles

GED Practice: Choosing Topic Sentences (page 42)

1. **b.** Many manufacturers try to increase sales by offering money-saving coupons or rebates.

2. **a.** An organization will reward people who report information about crimes that have been committed.

3. **a.** A résumé is a tool that can help you get a job interview.

GED Practice: Writing Topic Sentences (page 43)

There are many ways to write topic sentences for the paragraphs. Here are some examples:

1. More than ever before, adults need an education to succeed.

2. Smoking demands a price to one's health and one's wallet.

3. Getting out of debt may be difficult, but there are ways to do it.

4. Before you take a drug from your medicine cabinet, you should determine whether it is usable or not.

GED Practice: Writing Introductory Paragraphs (page 45)

There is more than one correct way to write each introductory paragraph. Share your work with your teacher or another student.

GED Practice: Writing Body Paragraphs (page 47)

There is more than one correct way to write each set of body paragraphs. Share your work with your teacher or another student.

GED Practice: Developing Body Paragraphs (page 49)

There are many ways to answer the questions. Here are some examples:

1. **Details:** Sweet, creamy chocolate tastes so good it should be a crime to eat it; it is better than winning.

2. **Details:** Leaving the world behind and escaping into sleep is vitally important to your health.

3. **Examples:** Car horns, engines, and other traffic sounds beep, roar, and chug along; refrigerators, fans, and other appliance motors hum, whir, and stir the air; people talking and yelling make yakking and shrieking noises; music from radios mixes with sounds from television sets.

4. **Examples:** Hurried people try to get ahead of you in line; they bump into you on the streets, on the subways, and in buses; they play music too loud and interrupt your thoughts.

There are many details and examples that could be added to the paragraphs. Share your work with your teacher or another student.

GED Practice: The Concluding Paragraph (pages 50–51)

There is more than one correct way to write each concluding paragraph. Share your work with your teacher or another student.

GED Review: Unit 3: Writing (pages 52–53)

There is more than one correct way to write the introductory paragraph, the body paragraphs, and the concluding paragraph for the topic assignment. Share your work with your teacher or another student.

Unit 4: Evaluating
GED Practice: Evaluating an Essay (page 58–70)

Answers will vary. Here are some possible responses.

1. A likely score is 2. The writer states a point of view and provides support for a main idea, but there is insufficient paragraph development for an essay. The sentence structure contains errors.

2. A likely score is 1. The essay lacks focus and has limited organization. It fails to give description and support for the point of view. The writer has difficulty with the conventions of English, and the errors distract significantly from the essay.

3. A likely score is 4. The essay has effective organization, but the paragraphs are not fully developed. It needs more support for the ideas in the second paragraph. Errors in the conventions of English are present; there are several run-on sentences.

4. A likely score is 6. The essay has effective organization with a clear thesis statement and topic sentences. It has strong examples that support the main ideas. The writer has good control of the conventions of English. The revisions and messiness of the essay do not detract from its score.

5. A likely score is 5. The essay has effective organization with a clear thesis statement and topic sentences. Several examples

are given to support topic sentences of the paragraphs. There are random errors in the conventions of English, but they do not distract the reader significantly.

6. A likely score is 4. The essay is well organized with a clear presentation of ideas. There is adequate support, but the language is too formal. There are some problems with sentence structure. The extra length of the essay does not earn it extra points.

GED Review: Unit 4: Evaluating (page 71)

Share your work with your teacher or another student.

UNIT 5: REVISING
GED Practice: Revising Your Ideas and Organization (page 76)

Delete sentences off topic: "I own a car and so does my brother." (paragraph 1) "My favorite is country music." (paragraph 3) "Bus riding is okay." (paragraph 5) "My brother and I rode the bus everywhere before we got our cars." (paragraph 5)

Add more details and examples: add to the second paragraph and the third paragraph.

GED Practice: Revising the Conventions of English (page 79)

Run-on sentence: The last sentence in paragraph 2 could be corrected like this: "In addition, they usually offer short menus. You can make a quick, easy decision about what you want to order."

Run-on sentence: The second sentence in paragraph 4 could be corrected like this: "The husband and wife are tired when they come home and don't want to cook. Instead, they want to spend time with their kids."

Sentence fragment: The second sentence in paragraph 3 could be corrected like this: "Hamburgers cost under a dollar."

Commas: Add commas to this series in the second sentence in paragraph 2: "near homes, by companies, and along highways."

Spelling: The following words are misspelled: It's (paragraph 1), finally (paragraph 4), therefore (paragraph 4), popularity (paragraph 5).

GED Practice: Revising an Essay (page 80)

Delete sentences off topic: "Financing a house is extremely expensive these days." (paragraph 2) "Every time I go to the bookstore I see all these books about travel." (paragraph 4)

Add more details and examples: add to the second body paragraph.

Sentence fragment: The second sentence in paragraph 3 could be corrected like this: "For example, cancer and AIDS research are charities that I would love to donate money to."

Run-on sentence: The fourth sentence in paragraph 4 could be corrected like this: "I would never cook another meal because I would eat out every day in a different restaurant."

Grammatical usage: The verb come in the first sentence should be comes.

Commas: Add commas to this series of phrases in the last sentence in paragraph 4: "every concert, every sports event, and every new movie."

Spelling: These words are misspelled: college (paragraph 2), different (paragraph 4).

Capitalization: The word state in sentence 2 should not be capitalized.

Punctuation: In sentence two of paragraph 2, parent's should be parents'. The last sentence in paragraph 5 needs a period.

GED Review: Unit 5: Revising (page 81)

Share your work with your teacher or another student.

UNIT 6: MORE ON PREWRITING
GED Practice: More Ways to Gather Ideas (pages 86–87)

There is more than one correct response. Share your work with your teacher or another student.

GED Practice: More Ways to Organize (page 90)

There is more than one correct response. Share your work with your teacher or another student.

GED Review: Unit 6: More on Prewriting (page 91)

Share your work with your teacher or another student.

UNIT 7: RAISING YOUR SCORE
GED Practice: Using Transitions (page 94)

The transitions are in heavy type.

Some people complain that they don't have enough leisure time. **Instead**, they should realize that more leisure time can have both good and bad effects upon their lives.

On one hand, more leisure time can improve the quality of many people's lives. They would have more time to spend with their families, to learn new things, to explore their creativity, and to travel. **As a result**, family relationships would improve. **Additionally**, people would become skilled in sports and hobbies.

On the other hand, too much leisure time can have some bad effects. People with little imagination or low self-esteem don't always do well with time on their hands. **In fact**, some people become depressed or bored. **Also**, some join gangs or get into trouble with the law.

In addition, more leisure time can be expensive **because** all leisure activities— taking courses, traveling, sports—cost money. **Moreover**, it probably means fewer working hours. **And** that means less pay.

There are good and bad points to having more leisure time. **However**, if I had a choice, I'd take the extra time off!

GED Practice: Including Facts and Opinions (page 96)

1. a. F   e. F
    b. O   f. F
    c. F   g. O
    d. O

2. There is more than one correct way to respond. Here are some examples:

    a. **Fact:** Movies have been a popular form of entertainment for decades.

    Opinion: The price of a movie is a bargain.

b. Fact: Attendance at sporting events increases every year.

Opinion: There's no better way to spend your entertainment dollar than at a baseball game.

c. Fact: A hobby such as hot-air ballooning is more expensive than one such as hiking.

Opinion: Everyone should take up a hobby.

GED Practice: Using Precise Words (page 98)

There is more than one correct way to respond. Here are some examples:

1. **a.** jammed, creeping, crawling, snarling, stinky, fumes, smog, stop and start movements, irritation, honking, yelling, bumper to bumper

   b. ringing, buzzing, instrument, tool, attention-grabbing, annoying, essential, nuisance, talking, listening, waiting, dialing, means of communication, long cord connecting one person to another

   c. crinkly, grimy, drab, green, essential, a must, problem solver, comforting, way to get things you want

   d. sunny, blue skies, parched ground, steamy, splashing water, shouting children, ice cream, watermelon, snow cones, swimming, ball playing, camping, horseback riding, hot and muggy, like an oven

2. **a.** Listening to music is relaxing.

   b. Raising a child is demanding.

   c. Crime is a serious problem.

d. Watching television can be habit-forming.

GED Review: Unit 7: Raising Your Score (page 99)

Share your work with your teacher or another student.

UNIT 8: POWER REVIEW
GED Practice: Evaluating and Revising (page 106)
Organization:

- Introductory paragraph—essay topic and thesis statement
- Body paragraphs—topic sentences and details related to the topic sentences
- Concluding paragraph—restates topic and reviews ideas
- Essay sticks to the topic

Support:

- Paragraphs include specific details and examples to support topic sentences
- Essay supports thesis statement

Clarity:

- Main idea understandable
- Supporting ideas expressed clearly

Conventions of English:

- Complete sentences
- Correct grammar
- Correct punctuation
- Correct spelling
- Capital letters

GED Practice: Your Writing Strategy (page 110)

Responses will vary. Share your work with your teacher or another student.

GED Practice: Scoring Your Essay (page 112)

Responses will vary. Share your work with your teacher or another student.

GED Practice: Unit 8: POWER Review (page 113)

Responses will vary. Share your work with your teacher or another student.

WRITER'S HANDBOOK
GED Practice: Sentence Fragments (page 122)

Answers will vary. Here are some possibilities.

1. It is hard getting out of the habit of smoking. Getting out of the habit of smoking is what I am working toward.

2. We are going to the movies this evening. Going to the movies this evening is my reward for a hard week's work.

3. We're going out to dinner after the Super Bowl Game. After the Super Bowl Game, I will clean up the family room.

4. The Dallas Cowboys and the New York Giants will play a game on Sunday. My favorite teams are the Dallas Cowboys and the New York Giants.

5. After playing baseball for several years, he opened a sporting goods store. She wants to play basketball after playing baseball for several years.

6. Both of their sons like sports and hobbies. She has no outside interests like sports and hobbies.

GED Practice: Run-on Sentences (page 124)

Answers will vary. Here are some possibilities.

1. The team had lost the game, so the players were not happy.

2. Most children do not go to school all year. They have vacation in the summer.

3. My mother likes movies, yet she does not like television very much.

4. My friend lived in Georgia, and she liked the warm weather.

5. Some people have many pets. Others have no pets at all.

6. I worked hard at my job, but I did not get a raise.

GED Practice: Capitalization (page 126)

1. Many, Bugs Bunny, Saturday

2. The, American, West

3. Today, I, New York, San Francisco

4. An, New York Times, Dr. Howard Bookman

5. School, November, December, Thanksgiving, Christmas

6. Do, The Adventures, Huckleberry Finn, The Waltons

7. The Humane Society

8. If, Boston City Council, Boston Symphony Orchestra, Michael Jackson

9. I, Dr. James Street

10. I, France, Arch, Triumph, Eiffel Tower

11. Aunt Kate, Thanksgiving

GED Practice: Commas (page 128)

1. Radio, television,

2. steep,

3. health, enjoy,

4. city,

5. Maple, Smithville,

6. Tuesday, September 8, 1986,

7. quickly,

8. pots, pans, dishes,

9. bread,

GED Practice: Apostrophes (page 128)

1. friend's, wasn't

2. Don't, car's

3. They're, programs'

4. lawyer's

5. workers'

6. We've

7. We'll, store's

8. He's, mother's

9. We're, family's

10. He's, son's

GED Practice: Spelling: Sound-Alike Words (page 130)

1. their, its

2. your, their

3. its, their, too

4. your, two

5. It's, your, you're

6. They're, it's, too, there

7. Two, to, too

8. It's, too, to

GED Practice: Spelling: Words with -ie and -ei (page 130)

1. weigh

2. nieces

3. received

4. eighth

5. seize

6. relieved

7. piece

8. weird

9. ceiling

10. friend, pierced

GED Practice: Spelling: Words with Suffixes (page 132)

1. dropping

2. hoping

3. dating

4. stopped

5. sitting

6. giving

7. robbed

8. swimming

9. hopped

10. cutting

GED Practice: Spelling: -y Words with Suffixes (page 132)

1. easily

2. tried

3. crying

4. supplying

5. reliable

6. laziness

7. satisfied

8. busier

9. fiftieth

10. delayed

Glossary

asking questions a technique to gather or expand ideas that involves asking who, what, when, where, why, or how about a given topic

background information factual material in the assigned topic for a GED essay; it gives historical or descriptive information that shows why the subject may involve several points of view

background sentences one or two sentences in the introduction of an essay that give general information about the topic to help introduce the reader to the topic

body paragraph one of the three paragraphs that make up the body of an essay; each body paragraph contains a topic sentence that is supported in the paragraph and in turn supports the essay's main idea

brainstorming a technique for gathering ideas in which a writer quickly jots down ideas about a given topic without evaluating them; after a set time, the writer evaluates the ideas and crosses out inappropriate ones

caret (^) an arrow-shaped punctuation mark used to show where words should be inserted in Revising an essay

cause and effect a relationship between actions: a cause is the reason something happens; an effect is the result set in motion by the cause

choosing your main idea part of the Planning step; a writer thinks about how he or she feels about a topic and decides what opinion or point of view to present in an essay

clarity a feature of writing that refers to how clearly ideas are presented and how well ideas are understood by the reader

compare and contrast a method of ordering ideas; to compare ideas, a writer shows how they are alike; to contrast ideas, a writer shows how they are different

composition an essay

concluding paragraph the last paragraph in a five-paragraph essay that sums up and reviews the information in the body

conventions of English rules for the use of written English; grammar, punctuation, capitalization, and word usage

details supporting ideas that back up the topic sentence of a paragraph

developing your body paragraphs part of the Writing step that involves giving details and examples to support the topic sentences

effects the results of a given cause; GED essay questions often ask writers to state the effects of something

essay a written composition that presents the writer's point of view about a topic; a typical five-paragraph essay includes an introduction, three body paragraphs, and a conclusion

evaluating the fourth step in the POWER writing program; it involves checking the presentation of ideas and the conventions of English

evaluating your ideas and organization part of the Evaluating step that uses organization, support, and clarity as criteria for assessing an essay

evaluating your use of the conventions of English part of the Evaluation process that relates to the mechanics and grammatical structure of an essay

examples instances that illustrate or represent what a writer wants to say; GED writing assignments may ask the writer to use examples to support a point of view

expanding your groups part of the Organizing step in writing an essay; it involves trying to add to the list of ideas by using methods such as asking questions or brainstorming

fact a statement that can be proved true by checking with a reliable source, such as a reference book

figuring out the topic part of the Planning step; figuring out the topic means analyzing the topic to determine what the subject of the written essay should be

five-paragraph essay the usual response to a GED writing assignment; a composition that contains five paragraphs—an introduction, three body paragraphs, and a conclusion

gathering ideas part of the Planning stage in which a writer lists or writes down related ideas about a topic to support a main idea

grouping ideas a way to organize related ideas so that the ideas in each group have something in common; since a five-paragraph essay requires three groups of related ideas, each group will become a supporting paragraph

holistic scoring the method of scoring an essay used by GED scorers; an essay is judged on its overall effectiveness

idea circle a way to generate ideas by noting how widening groups of people are affected by something; three nested rings relate to the writer personally, the people close to the writer, and society at large

idea map a way to record ideas that shows their relationship to the main idea; it involves circling ideas and connecting them to the main idea with lines

instructions part of the writing assignment that tells the kind of information a writer needs to give in an essay; the instructions ask the writer to agree or disagree and give specific examples to back up ideas

introductory paragraph the first paragraph of an essay; it includes the essay topic and introduces the main idea

issue the part of a topic assignment that addresses the results or consequences of something happening

key words words in the instructions that help a writer understand what to write; for example, *state a view*, or *explain how*

labeling a method of naming groups of ideas; each label becomes the topic sentence for a paragraph

listing a technique for gathering ideas in which a writer jots down ideas in the order he or she thinks of them

logical order ordering ideas in a way that seems appropriate for the kinds of ideas presented

main idea the opinion about a topic that a writer presents in an essay or composition

mapping a visual way to organize ideas by showing the relationships between ideas; idea groups are connected to the main idea with lines; ideas, details, and examples are then connected to the idea groups

mechanics of writing capitalization and punctuation

naming ideas part of the Organizing step in which a label is given to a group of ideas to show what they have in common

numbering groups determining an order for groups of ideas and numbering them 1, 2, and 3 for the three paragraphs of the essay

opinion a statement of preference or belief; a point of view about a topic; it may include a writer's ideas, feelings, and attitudes about a subject; an opinion may include value judgments

order of importance a method of ordering groups of ideas in which the usual order is to build from weakest to strongest idea so that the last idea is the most important point

ordering your groups part of the Organizing step; groups of ideas are ordered to give a logical progression of ideas for the subject matter; for a GED essay, there are two useful methods of ordering groups—order of importance, and compare and/or contrast

organization a feature of good writing; ideas are put together and ordered logically so that a reader is able to understand how the writer sees the ideas in relation to one another

organizing the second step of the POWER writing process; Organizing involves dividing ideas into three groups, adding strong ideas to the groups, and putting the idea groups in logical order

outlining a method of Organizing ideas that shows how ideas relate to each other; in an outline, numbers and letters identify ideas and show how they are classified and ranked

paragraph a division of a written composition that is organized around a main idea; it usually has a topic sentence that tells its main idea, and it usually begins with an indented line

planning the first step of the POWER writing program; it involves figuring out the topic, understanding the instructions, choosing a main idea, and gathering ideas for the essay

POWER Steps the five steps for producing an effective five-paragraph essay in response to a GED writing assignment—**P**lanning, **O**rganizing, **W**riting, **E**valuating, and **R**evising

precise words words that give the reader a clear mental picture of the ideas a writer wants to present; they often appeal to the five senses

preview sentences sentences in the introductory paragraph that tell the reader what to expect in an essay; preview sentences are brief and general

prewriting the Planning and Organizing steps in writing an essay

proofreading part of the Evaluation process that involves looking over the essay to determine if the conventions of English have been followed

pros and cons advantages and disadvantages of something

reasons facts about an issue that tell why or how it occurs

related ideas ideas that are connected in some way to each other; related ideas are grouped together to become supporting paragraphs

revising the last step in the POWER writing program; it involves changing the parts of an essay that are weak to create a stronger, more effective essay; it is a two-step process that requires correcting the ideas and organization and then correcting the conventions of English

revising your ideas and organization part of the Revising step that involves changing the organization, support, and clarity of an essay by adding, reordering, or deleting ideas

revising your use of the conventions of English part of the Revising step that involves fixing any incorrect grammar, capitalization, punctuation, or word usage

revision methods (marks) a way to show corrections on an essay: cross out unwanted words; add additional words in the margin or between the lines; use carets to show where additions are inserted

run-on sentence two sentences put together as if they were only one sentence; a run-on sentence can be corrected in two ways: by making two sentences with a period and a capital or by adding a comma followed by a conjunction between the two sentences

sensory words words that use the five senses—sight, hearing, taste, smell, and touch—in descriptions; sensory words help a writer get across ideas in vivid and interesting ways

sentence a group of words that expresses a complete thought; it contains a subject and a verb

sentence fragment an incomplete sentence; a group of words that does not express a complete thought but ends with a period; it can be corrected by adding a subject or a verb to complete the sentence or by adding the fragment to another complete sentence

subject the part of a sentence that tells who or what does the action

support the ideas a writer gathers to back up an essay's main idea

supporting paragraphs the three body paragraphs that provide support for the main idea of an essay

thesis statement a sentence that states the topic of an essay; it is usually the last sentence in the introductory paragraph; a thesis statement may be written by expanding the main idea

three parts of an essay an essay has three basic parts that each serve a specific function in the essay—the introduction, body, and conclusion

topic the subject matter of an essay; the issue or problem that a writer addresses

topic assignment the designated topic or subject to write about for the GED essay

topic sentence a sentence in a paragraph that tells the main idea of the paragraph; each well-developed paragraph contains a topic sentence, either at the beginning, middle, or end

transitions words or phrases that help connect one idea to the next; transitions help make ideas clear and emphasize organization; they show how ideas relate to one another

understanding the instructions part of the Planning step; the writer plans what to write by determining what the instructions say and what the instructions ask of the writer

writing the third step in the POWER writing program; a writer writes an essay by composing the five paragraphs that include the introduction, body, and conclusion

writing assignment the designated essay question to write about for the GED; it includes the topic, background information about the topic, and instructions on how and what to write about

writing your body paragraphs part of the Writing step that involves backing up the thesis statement in the introductory paragraph with three supporting body paragraphs

writing your concluding paragraph part of the Writing step that requires a writer to restate the topic and review the ideas from the essay

writing your introductory paragraph part of the Writing step that involves stating the topic and the main idea of the essay, adding preview statements of the ideas to be presented, and providing background information

Index

≡Answer Sheet

Name: _____ **Class:** _____ **Date:** _____

_____

_____

_____

_____

_____

_____

_____

_____

_____

_____

_____

_____

_____

_____

_____

_____

_____

_____

_____

_____

_____

Continue your essay on next page

USE A BALL POINT PEN TO WRITE YOUR ESSAY

DO NOT

MARK

IN THIS

AREA

_____

_____

_____

_____

_____

_____

_____

_____

_____

_____

_____

_____

_____

_____

_____

_____

_____

_____

_____

_____

MAKE NO MARKS IN THIS AREA

○○○○○○○○○○○○○○○○○○○○○○○○▣